PRAISE FOR

DAVID SCOTT PETERS & RESTAURANT PROSPERITY FORMULA™

"Finally, a resource that gives you a no-BS, simple-to-follow plan for restaurant success! David's no-nonsense approach strips down all the excuses and doubts in our heads as operators and then gives you the paint-by-numbers plan to make real change in your restaurant. The systems that are outlined in this book are both relevant and practical on their own, but David takes it a step further by teaching you how to implement them in your business and whom you need on your team to be successful. It's refreshing to learn and get advice from a true restaurant expert who knows how to walk the walk from his own successes and trip-ups in the industry, instead of from some academic type that has never worked a day in the restaurant trenches.

"Whether you're a rookie that's just getting started in the business or a seasoned veteran looking to take your business to the next level, this book is for you!"

—BRAD HACKERT, DIRECTOR OF RESTAURANT OPERATIONS, FLORA-BAMA

"Without a doubt the systems that David Scott Peters teaches are a bottom line changer for any foodservice business. You cannot afford not to read this book if you want to be a profitable restaurant owner or caterer, and I know this from firsthand knowledge."

—SANDY KOREM, OWNER, THE FESTIVE KITCHEN; FOUNDER, THE CATERING COACH

"Are you making the absolute maximum profit for your type of restaurant? Say what? Fact is, the proper prime cost, budget, and P&L systems that guarantee a healthy bank account for your specific restaurant concept are not publicly available. But they are attainable. And don't worry, David's gift for turning complexity into simplicity is unmatched. Inside these pages, he breaks mind-numbing concepts into bite-sized, step-by-step processes that anyone can follow. Think of this book as your personal, one-of-a-kind treasure map with a clearly marked path and a big X where the gold is. Bring your shovel because you'll be doing some digging."

—KAMRON KARINGTON, FOUNDER AND CEO, REPEAT RETURNS

RESTAURANT PROSPERITY FORMULA™

RESTAURANT

WHAT SUCCESSFUL

PROSPERITY

RESTAURATEURS DO

FORMULA™

DAVID SCOTT PETERS

Published by Advantage, Charleston, South Carolina.
Member of Advantage Media Group.

Restaurant Prosperity Formula is a registered trademark. ADVANTAGE is a registered trademark, and the Advantage colophon is a trademark of Advantage Media Group, Inc.

Printed in the United States of America.

10 9 8 7 6 5 4 3 2 1

ISBN: 978-1-64225-039-8
LCCN: 2019919235

Cover and Layout design by David Taylor.

This publication is designed to provide accurate and authoritative information in regard to the subject matter covered. It is sold with the understanding that the publisher is not engaged in rendering legal, accounting, or other professional services. If legal advice or other expert assistance is required, the services of a competent professional person should be sought.

 Advantage Media Group is proud to be a part of the Tree Neutral® program. Tree Neutral offsets the number of trees consumed in the production and printing of this book by taking proactive steps such as planting trees in direct proportion to the number of trees used to print books. To learn more about Tree Neutral, please visit **www.treeneutral.com**.

Advantage Media Group is a publisher of business, self-improvement, and professional development books and online learning. We help entrepreneurs, business leaders, and professionals share their Stories, Passion, and Knowledge to help others Learn & Grow. Do you have a manuscript or book idea that you would like us to consider for publishing? Please visit **advantagefamily.com** or call **1.866.775.1696**.

To restaurant owners everywhere, who fuel our communities and our economy.

CONTENTS

FOREWORD

By Anne Gannon, CPA
Founder and principal
The Largo Group
www.TheLargoGroup.com

I am so excited you are reading this book! You have picked such a great resource to put you on the path to making incredible changes in your business. No one can match David Scott Peters's enthusiasm, experience, and results.

I came to know David Scott Peters in 2017 when we were both presenters at a restaurant and lodging trade show. We were both there as education speakers. I was teaching a session on restaurant accounting, and David was there to teach a couple of sessions to help restaurant owners lower food cost and hold their management teams accountable. I could not believe how many people attended his sessions. Turns out his reputation preceded him, and restaurant owners and managers filled the seats and lined the walls for fifty-five minutes of his expertise.

I was immediately impressed by his approach to the restaurant business. I noticed a striking difference from other coaches and consultants in that he's not afraid to tackle the hard stuff and get restaurant owners to fix their issues. It's not always what they want to hear. He points them toward the hard decisions to help them reach their goals. He doesn't use buzzwords, which is very common with "consultants," unless four-letter words are buzzwords in the restaurant industry.

David covers all aspects of the business, from leadership to motivating employees to the ins and outs of the business. He used to say that if you let him into your restaurant, he could find $10,000 in hidden profits somewhere between the front door and the back door. It's not an exaggeration; I've seen him uncover much more than $10,000 in an initial review of a restaurant's operations.

Aside from helping restaurant owners get a handle on their operations, the real gift David gives them is control over their own destinies. He teaches them that they have the power in their businesses regardless of what's happening with the economy or the industry. They are in charge of their managers, their food orders, their menus, and their servers. They make the decisions, and those who don't fall in line aren't good for the business and must go.

A few months after meeting him at the trade show, I had the honor of meeting his coaching clients at a quarterly meeting. I saw firsthand the life-changing impact he had on people's lives and their businesses. The meeting was in Chicago during a time that is considered a busy season for most restaurants. Not only were these restaurant owners not in their businesses, they were enjoying extra time away to enjoy the city. They were joking about staying in better hotels and taking great vacations. It was a stark contrast to anything I'd ever seen after working in the hospitality business. In an industry where 62 percent of all restaurant businesses will fail in their first three years, seeing the success of those who follow David's process made it obvious that there was something special and different about what they're doing. Going to that meeting and sitting in a room with entrepreneurs who had really achieved the entrepreneurial dream was very inspiring.

These business owners were from all sorts of different locations, backgrounds, and experiences, and they ran a variety of restaurant styles. The common denominator was implementing the systems that David taught them and then holding themselves accountable to them.

David's impact on those business owners' lives eventually spilled over into my business. He and I found we held a similar business philosophy that was more about partnering with businesses and being an extension of their business than about just throwing down some solutions and leaving business owners on their own to figure it all out. Because of this shared philosophy, he began referring restaurant owners to my accounting firm. Owners trusted him so completely that when I'd call them to "sell" them on my firm, they would often cut me off and tell me that David had sent them, and therefore they were ready to do business with me, no questions asked. These referrals had a huge impact on the growth of my own business.

What David offers is bigger than just running a successful restaurant. Those who follow what David teaches experience a better business and a better life. My hope for you—with this book in your hand—is that you will one day be one of those restaurant owners who can take great vacations and stay in nicer hotels. If you follow what David teaches and you persevere, I know you can.

THE DAVID SCOTT PETERS STORY

I only have one mission: to help independent restaurant owners—from single to multiunit operations—not only survive but *thrive* in the sea of chain restaurants that dominate our industry. For as long as I can remember, my dream has been to put my knowledge and experience to work while revolutionizing the way independent restaurants operate.

Consider today my "mission accomplished" moment.

I'm the expert. It's a title I've earned after years of busting my ass to learn the ins and outs of our industry. When I launched my first business, TheRestaurantExpert.com, I set off on a new mission to train my members until they operated their restaurants like experts too. For every restaurant we worked with, the assignment was to accomplish three main goals:

- simplify the restaurant's operations,

- start making more money than ever before, and

- bring balance back to the owner's life to allow them to enjoy the benefits of the first two goals.

Sound good? You're damn right it does! That mission and those goals drove me for sixteen years, and it worked.

Proven Expertise

You're in for a real treat because what I'm offering is so much more than a book. I'm about to take you through the most comprehensive restaurant owner manual you've ever read. Even better, I'm sharing some exclusive readers-only content as *free*miums that'll help you get started right away. I'm not one of those speakers who likes to lead you in with a dollar on a string—I teach! Listen, I'd never set you up for failure, and my track record literally speaks for itself. I can help anyone with any type of restaurant anywhere in the world. I've proven it.

I've been invited to serve as a featured speaker at prominent industry events like the National Restaurant Show in Chicago, the International Restaurant and Foodservice Show of New York, the Florida Restaurant and Lodging Show, the Western Foodservice and Hospitality Expo, the Nightclub and Bar Show in Las Vegas, Pizza Expo—I can really do this all day!

My passion for the independent owner has been spread through top publications in the industry like *Nation's Restaurant News, Restaurant Hospitality, Restaurant Startup and Growth,* and *Nightclub and Bar Magazine.*

I'm honored to see how far my passion and commitment have carried me over the years, and here, I plan to share my expertise to totally disrupt the way you manage your business.

A Snapshot of Success

Experience is, and always will be, the best teacher you'll ever have. Nothing I teach was learned overnight. It took years of trial and error (and surviving the gauntlet you're tossed into when your mom is the first manager you've ever worked under) before I could confidently make the promises I make today.

Good, bad, or toxic as hell, I took something valuable away from every position I've ever held. You'll see a lot of those stories in the pages to come, but I just thought I'd share a little timeline to help you follow along. I've been busy for the last couple of decades so don't blink—you might miss something important.

Let's take a quick walk down memory lane ...

June 2019

I launched an online training company, DavidScottPeters.com, for restaurant owners, managers, and operators. The curriculum is centered around my trademarked Restaurant Prosperity Formula, which encapsulates everything I've learned after thirty years in the restaurant business about what it takes to run a successful restaurant. It doesn't matter if it's a mom-and-pop independent, a multiunit independent operation, or a small franchise group. The Restaurant Prosperity Formula is the path to success for restaurants.

July 2003

TheRestaurantExpert.com was founded. We evolved over the years, and hearing success stories from my past members still hits a soft spot. Thousands of restaurant owners increased their profits by an average of $4,000–$8,000 per month using everything they learned at our semiannual workshops, at one-on-one trainings, and through direct coaching using SMART (simple, measurable, applicable, repeatable, and trainable) Systems Pro, the online management software I developed to automate the systems that were the focus of the coaching and training.

October 1997–July 2005

Famous Sam's, Inc., a thirty-one-unit restaurant and sports bar chain out of Mesa, Arizona, gave me a taste of what independents were doing wrong (and of how chains can self-sabotage too). Unit sales across the system topped $30 million annually, and still, the business found a way to tap dance around bankruptcy.

I served as the director of operations from 1997 to 1999 before moving into independent consulting for a little over a year. When the shit hit the fan—see the bankruptcy reference above—Famous Sam's asked me back to be the chief operating officer and director to resolve their legal issues and turn the business around so it would be fit to sell. I orchestrated a system-wide rebranding initiative that saved the business, and then I stuck things out until I made good on my promise to sell the company within five years.

January 1999–October 1999

Scottsdale Culinary Institute in Scottsdale, Arizona, introduced me to a new love. Being a manager was one thing, but I never realized how satisfying teaching would be. I created lesson plans that taught my students how to manage and run restaurants based on real-world experience. Between management and human resources and wines and spirits, I learned how to transfer everything I'd learned into a new skill.

May 1993–October 1997

Coyote Springs Brewing Company and Café taught me to push myself more than ever before. I was hired as a bartender, then worked my way up to bar manager. The owners started to recognize my potential, so I was promoted to restaurant manager. Tasked with developing staff and coordinating the start-up of our second location, Coyote Springs forced me to adapt to my surroundings and step up to challenges every day.

By December of '95, I was promoted to operations manager, which meant I was responsible for overseeing both locations, with $3.5 million in combined annual sales. With 10 managers and 110-plus line employees under my direction, I developed budgets and created systems to automate our daily operations. By the time I was done, our cost of goods sold (COGS) margin had decreased by more than 15 percent.

Long before I ever stepped foot in Coyote Springs, passion for the hospitality industry pumped through my veins. I grew up working in Friar Tuck's Tavern, my family's restaurant and catering business.

> My mom was my manager, and she never thought twice about handing my ass to me.

My mom was my manager, and she never thought twice about handing my ass to me. Even after that, I was an underage dishwasher gambling with my life, mopping with a deadly combination of bleach and ammonia in a local Italian restaurant. Listen—don't ask any questions. All you need to know is common sense isn't very common at all.

Moving on.

Between all the bars and restaurants I worked at while trying to pick up women in college and everything else I learned along the way, I'll say it again, I'm *the expert*—the question is, Are you ready to make the commitment?

I Want You to Be My Next Greatest Achievement

Even with my résumé laid out in black and white, it always feels incomplete. I know there's somebody else out there, another restaurant owner who needs my help before they give up on their dream. Before you make that decision, before you continue to leave money on the table at the end of each month, just give me ten minutes of your time.

I've been doing this for so long, I can probably guess what's on your mind. I know firsthand that running a restaurant is hard work. We're in one of the most difficult businesses to run. I feel your pain;

in fact, I'm reminded of those struggles on a daily basis.

1. Food cost is out of control.

2. Labor cost is killing me.

3. My people are *idiots*.

4. My managers won't do anything.

It doesn't matter how long you've been in business or how many restaurants you own; I bet something on that list sounds familiar. Earlier, I asked for your commitment. You give me that, and I promise to help you turn things around.

As you read, you'll eventually learn that I'm a man who appreciates specifics. No detail is too big or too small. For clarity, let's go over exactly what types of commitment I'm looking for and what you'll need to be successful.

- **Committed to change.** When you really get into the swing of things and start implementing the systems I suggest, you'll find some of your people aren't as open to change. Many people get bit by the "if it ain't broke, don't fix it" bug, and those are the very same people who'll run your restaurant into the ground.

> When you shift your culture to focus on profits, everyone benefits in the long run.

- **Committed to changing your company culture.** Running a profitable restaurant isn't a luxury. It's your responsibility. If you don't succeed, everyone suffers—from the guests to the employees and even you and your family. When you shift your culture to focus on profits, everyone benefits in the long run.

- **Committed to investing your time.** As I mentioned earlier, you don't gain experience overnight. The solutions I'm about to share will take time to bear fruit. It takes a lot of man hours to start putting these systems in place; implementation, training, monitoring, and coaching demand a sizeable investment. There's no magic pill for success.

- **Committed in your mindset.** You must be willing to do whatever it takes. Change in your restaurant starts with the head of the dragon. Without your determination, nothing will happen. Your commitment to change needs to be so strong that you'll be willing to either convince your people to jump on board or replace some good workers with someone more trainable.

- **Committed financially.** You have to hire the management you need and give up your need to be in the restaurant 24-7. You have to invest in the systems and technology your restaurant needs to get the job done quickly and efficiently.

I need all five commitments from you—you can't slack in any area or else our plan fails from the beginning. Without this level of commitment, you risk falling into Einstein's definition of insanity: doing the same thing over and over again while expecting a different result.

There are ten ideas every restaurateur must practice to gain full advantage of what I call the *Restaurant Prosperity Formula*—the recipe to achieving success on all levels:

1. core values,

2. organizational chart communication,

3. responsibility to be profitable,

4. imposing your will,

5. cash controls and checklists,

6. budgets and recipe costing cards,

7. prime cost,

8. finding an implementor,

9. taking action, and

10. getting "good" help.

Implementing these practices will put more money in the bank; more importantly, they show you how to regain your freedom.

You deserve to have a life! With a management team in place and employees who know what the job is, how to do it, how well it should be done, and more importantly, by when, you'll finally see what it means to work *on* your business, not in it.

CHAPTER 1

DREAMS ARE MADE TO ORDER

"Suck it up, buttercup."

That was all I got. I'm not sure what response I was searching for—but that certainly wasn't it. This was back when I was thirteen years old. A waitress stiffed me on my tips, and I went running to my mom, who was also my boss, whining about what happened.

"She didn't tip me!" I bitched and moaned for as long as I could, desperately searching for *something* from her. It could've been empathy or understanding—maybe a little of both.

Maybe I thought she'd force her hand over the woman who ran off with my hard-earned money. I mean, I *was* the boss's son. But none of those things ever happened.

"Suck it up" was all my mom had to offer. She listened to my rant for as long as she could stand, then looked me dead in the eye and told me she wasn't going to do anything about it. Her only advice to me was "Work harder."

> It's not about how many years of experience you have; it's about what kind of experience you have.

Hard work was the first life lesson I ever learned. Many of my earliest memories revolve around the hustle and bustle of the restaurant world. I went from serving as an underage dishwasher at Lombardi's, a local Italian restaurant, to filling in as a dedicated laborer in our family business. As you'd imagine, being forced to juggle the fast-paced lifestyle that comes with running an independent restaurant was a lot for a young boy to deal with. Living in a world where your mom was your manager *first*, before any other role she served, was a tough pill to swallow. It wasn't until I got older and started to see what it meant to have thick skin that I really understood the value in those experiences.

Experience is always the best teacher. Unlike most people, getting into the restaurant industry wasn't a choice for me—I was born into hospitality.

Where most of us cherish childhood memories surrounding tire swings and beach vacations, many of mine involve tackling towers of dirty dishes. When I was coming up, dishwashing wasn't just a chore—it was an obligation. It was one of many responsibilities that helped sustain my family's business.

I was more than a son; I was an employee. A team member. My mom was more than a nurturing caregiver. She was a no-nonsense manager who didn't take any shit. Even to this day, she still reigns as the toughest manager I've ever known. As a teenager, I hated her unforgiving tactics. Now I realize she was molding me to confidently step into the cutthroat, high-intensity world of a restaurateur.

Ditching the Excuses

As a restaurant systems expert, I've had the privilege of working with restaurant owners from all walks of life. I've spent more than sixteen years perfecting my approach. Learning from restaurant owners, innovating systems, facilitating one-on-one coaching and training sessions—it's all earned me the right to call myself *the expert*.

Even before I realized my mission as a coach and trainer, before I learned the true meaning of those foundational values and principles instilled in me by my mom, before I found myself battling towers of dishes at Lombardi's, and before I figured out how to manage all the different personality types we encounter every day, I understood one overarching life lesson:

Excuses are useless.

Excuses weren't allowed in my family's restaurant. My mother worked her ass off from open to close, serving double duty as owner and manager, so she didn't have time for unnecessary shit. With me and my sister, you'd never see any sort of favoritism. For one, there weren't enough hours in the day to waste on coddling us. Number two, that just wasn't the way we were brought up.

If anything, my mom always pushed us harder than anyone else. If something needed to be done, we figured it out. I played whatever role I was asked. Dishwasher. Prep cook. Busboy.

Friar Tuck's Tavern gave me the confidence to excel in an environment that wouldn't allow me to fold. That was *our* business. A family business. Anything short of success wasn't an option. Under my mother's guidance, I developed the skills I needed to elevate in every possible area. Because of those foundational values and beliefs, I developed a remarkable reputation for myself everywhere I've worked since then.

I was always the youngest person sitting at the top of the food chain. I always kept my competition, friendly or otherwise, on their toes. Everyone has always kept one eye keenly focused on me. And that's largely because when it's time for me to work, I work—and cut out all the excuses.

If you can promise to do the same, I'll do all I can to provide you with the tools you need to whip your restaurant into tiptop shape. I don't care if you're operating your very first hot dog stand or if you have locations sprinkled across the nation—the founding principles you need to follow remain the same:

- Establish solid core values.

- Develop tailor-made operational systems.

- Train your people, and hold them accountable.

To make this work, you need to accept this challenge as a packaged deal. You can't master your restaurant's success without perfecting all three of these components. I don't care if you've been struggling in one area or if you think you've already mastered them all. By the time you finish this book, you'll know exactly what you need to do to run your business in a way that most independents can only dream of.

Chasing Failure with a Shot of Success

For the last two decades, I've traveled the corners of the globe speaking in front of audiences of all sizes. I've attracted a dedicated group of restaurateurs who rely on me to provide them with as much guidance and direction as they need to turn their businesses into well-oiled machines. Of all my years in the industry, and everything I've had my hands in while I've been building this reputation, one of the greatest assets I offer my restaurant owners is the fact that I get it.

Between all the tools, training, and resources I've developed over the years, I'm 100 percent sure that the best thing I will ever lay out on the table is my unquestioned understanding.

I've been there and done that.

There isn't a single complaint, issue, dilemma, or cause for concern that I haven't experienced on my own. There's nothing you can share with me that I haven't already dealt with or successfully coached a restaurateur through. I can promise results because I've developed a fail-proof set of systems that can carry any type of restaurant through whatever type of growth or market changes it may experience. And I've put it to the test time and again.

> I've been there and done that.
> There isn't a single complaint, issue, dilemma, or cause for concern that I haven't experienced on my own.

When you're done learning from me, you won't even need me anymore. But I'm not going anywhere. My number won't change, and you can still call me whenever you have a question. *Shit happens.* We all know that. But my systems are designed to teach you and your employees how to manage your own operation without depending on anybody.

I've seen how successful owners become after following my lead. I get calls and letters and emails from restaurant owners sharing their stories every single day. I know these processes work.

Are you ready to see them work for you? That's the real question.

Are you ready to put the past and the excuses behind you? Are you ready to wipe the slate clean and transform not just your operation but also your way of thinking? I plan to dig in and dig up everything that's prevented you from running your restaurant in a way that'll make it as profitable as possible.

The way my mom pushed me shaped my life forever. I used to think she was breeding me to be a good worker; now I understand that I was being coached to become an even greater leader.

The last few years have taught me something else about excuses. Do you know what they really do? Excuses mask the truth. That's what happened to me in college. I almost forgot some of the most valuable lessons my mother taught me. I was enrolled at Northeastern University, and no matter how hard I tried, I couldn't shake my ties to the hospitality industry.

I spent my holiday breaks hosting for a small restaurant behind Symphony Hall. I was working as the doorman at two bars; Maxwell Jumps was a bar right on campus with a small menu, and Seaside Grill was a restaurant and bar over in Faneuil Hall Marketplace in downtown Boston. I had a lot on my plate at the time. I was attending school on an athletic scholarship for rowing. When I stopped competing, I took a job as a doorman to earn some extra cash. I had two things on my mind: get a job in the industry and find an easy way to meet women! Hey, what do you expect? It was college. Can you blame me?

I will say this: back then, staying focused was even harder because the leadership I was under really sucked. I tried talking myself out of my interest in the industry. There wasn't any order or direction. Workers weren't being trained on what was expected of them. There weren't any systems in place. It was a mess.

Then, when I graduated from college, I worked as a restaurant manager for the Hyatt Regency on the Charles River for a very short time. It was so ugly there that—and I'm embarrassed to share this— it was the first and only time in my career when I actually walked off the job and quit without any notice.

I started to think hospitality just wasn't for me.

We all fight with the thought of walking away from it all. The chaos of the industry almost pushed me out the door, but for some reason, I just couldn't do it. I kept finding my way back.

Culture Is the First Course: The Coyote Springs Story

Let me be blunt. I'm not a chef—not in the least bit. I can pour you a stiff drink, but I can barely boil water without creating a mess. If you're looking for a leader to help you sauté and season, then I'm not your guy. Cooking may not be my forte, but I can open your eyes to something far more important to the success of your business.

I'm successful because with the right systems in place, I can run any kitchen. In the restaurant industry, culture outranks culinary expertise. I know some of you probably think I've lost my mind, but I'm standing on my word on this one. You'll see what I mean as you keep reading, but just think about this for a second:

You can whip up some of the tastiest food in the world, but if your restaurant is run with a bullshit culture, nobody's going to tolerate the atmosphere long enough to get plates on the table.

> The love-hate relationship I developed with hospitality was mainly due to the crappy cultures I dealt with while I was coming up.

The love-hate relationship I developed with hospitality was mainly due to the crappy cultures I dealt with while I was coming up. Fortunately, I had the pleasure of working with one company that proved that poor culture was the exception, not the rule to follow.

Sometimes, we need to be pushed into our destiny. Hard

work at my family's business and crazy experiences throughout my college career were only the beginning. My real "push" happened when I started working for a brewpub in Phoenix, Arizona, called Coyote Springs Brewing Company and Café. Thanks to the culture I witnessed there, I remembered how much I really loved the restaurant business.

Before I knew it, I was back behind the bar, and I must admit, I had bartending locked down. I was best in the world, and no one could convince me otherwise, not even now.

Here's a curveball for you: while I was coming up in the restaurant world, I started dipping my toes into improv comedy. Let me tell you, if there was anything that could tear me away from being behind the bar, it was the chance to step on stage and make people laugh.

I thought improv was going to carry me for the long haul back in those days, so I used bartending sort of like my stage beyond the stage. If I wasn't entertaining a crowd with one of my *Whose Line Is It Anyway?* bits, the bar gave me another audience that really loved me.

That was such a magical experience.

I'm still so grateful for the Garrards, the owners of Coyote Springs, for giving me that opportunity. What I witnessed was proof of how quickly a positive company culture can improve a restaurant's operations. It also lifted the veil on the flip side of that coin—a part of the story I never expected.

Bill Garrard was a retired banker who lived to work in his restaurant. Creating the best experience for his guests was all he ever focused on. He was lost in what I like to call the social worker leadership style, the approach for leaders who focus everything they do on the guest and their team. Social worker owners often ignore their numbers, which puts their restaurants on the path to have great Yelp reviews and negative bank accounts.

So Coyote Springs gave me an opportunity to shift back into a management role. Working as a bar manager, while bartending for the thrill, was an experience in itself.

I was there. I was always ready to roll up my sleeves and jump in wherever I was needed, even if that meant losing some sleep to help cover babysitting the hood cleaners overnight or anything else you can think of. I was present. I showed up and was always focused on making things happen. To me, that was the only thing that mattered.

I was killing the game, serving as a restaurateur superstar. Things were moving along so well, Bill decided to pull the general manager (GM) to the side to say, "Bring David on as a full-time manager."

The GM nearly had a heart attack and he was like "No freakin' way! We don't have the money for it." What Bill said next completely ripped apart my perspective:

"If David does his job, he's gonna pay for himself."

How many of us are taught to look at our talent as an asset, a valuable contribution to the bottom line of the business? Even in my small role, Bill saw me as *human capital*. He knew giving me the space to expand my horizon would be equally beneficial. He trusted that I'd help scale up the business—and that's exactly what I did, eventually being promoted into the operations manager position and overseeing our two locations.

Talk about the importance of company culture.

From there, I worked my way up the hospitality ladder until I was the director of operations for a franchisor of a sports bar chain with thirty-plus locations called Famous Sam's Restaurant and Sports Bar. Then I was an instructor at the Scottsdale Culinary Institute, teaching management and human resources and wines and spirits. Life happened, and I ended up accepting an offer to head *back* to Famous Sam's as the chief operating officer tasked to turn the company around from near bankruptcy to its ultimate sale. I worked in the midst of the action, behind the scenes, and just about every role in between. Today, I hold the greatest title I've ever maintained. Not because I am my own boss and run my own company. Not because I have an awesome family of amazing team players helping me along the way. Not because I've sat beside some of the most ambitious restaurant owners in the world and helped them see their businesses from a totally different perspective. Because I get to help.

I'm in the position to use my experiences to help independent owners materialize their goals. I get to help people build their legacies and operate their restaurants in a way that models day-to-day operations after the most successful chain businesses in the world.

As a restaurant industry expert coaching restaurant owners, operators, and managers, I have the opportunity to sit down with regular people and make their wildest dreams come true. Now, in this book, I am sharing this information to give you the same perspective and support.

Following the Message

I'm going to show you how to use systems and tools just like the ones chain restaurants use without losing your independence. My advice is outlined through a detailed, step-by-step synopsis of what you should've been doing yesterday if you want to keep your restaurant from continuously bleeding money.

First, we'll discuss the basic formula for success: systems. The profitability of your restaurant depends on how well you understand the need to have systems in place for *everything*. Nothing's too large or too small. Nothing's to be left to common sense. (Most people don't have any anyway.) Systems give you power and freedom; they let you impose your will in your restaurant without the need for you to be there.

Once we get that key concept down, we're going to move into what everyone really wants to know—how to get the job done. I'm going to show you how to create the systems your restaurant needs. Before you're finished reading, you'll know exactly what to do to identify the most important systems for your restaurant. Then I'll show you how to implement them while holding your people accountable for their actions.

The process is simple, but it'll only work if you place some extra emphasis on that last line. You have to hold your people accountable. It's the only way the rest of the steps will work together to help you reconcile the small but costly mistakes that usually capsize most independent restaurants. With this book, I'm giving you the keys to restaurant success and laying it all out on the line. I'm not just showing you what's possible. I'm about to walk you through each step, giving you as much guidance as I can.

Restaurant Prosperity Formula™—*What Successful Restaurateurs Do* would've turned into a couple of volumes if I shared everything I wanted to share. So, to make sure you walk away with a truckload of information, I'm backing this book up with a series of webinars and training courses to help guide you through each step. I'll help you revise every facet of your business—from your core values to your budget. Now that you have this book, you officially don't have any room to make excuses anymore.

By the time it's all said and done, you'll know why you need these systems, how to use them, and how *easy* it is for you to succeed. Once you see how your business transforms when your systems are up and running—and working together—you'll wonder why the hell it took you so long to get on board.

Don't get me wrong—this is work! Hard work. And a hell of a lot of it. The hardest part of this transition isn't what you may think. It's not controlling food cost or reducing your labor cost or even getting your freedom back—the hardest part of utilizing systems is getting people to use them every day. That's why company culture is the first thing I address.

CHAPTER TAKEAWAYS

- Ditch the excuses!

- Company culture defines your future success.

- This is hard work—but systems make it that much easier.

CHAPTER 2

BINGEING ON EXPERIENCE

When it comes to experience, I have more than enough to share. And somehow, things always come back around to strong company culture—or how strong it should have been. Let's look back to my time served as the assistant manager at the Hyatt Regency Cambridge in Massachusetts. I was twenty-two years old, fresh out of college, and only on the job for three months before I realized I was working in a hellhole.

My boss, the GM of the three-meal dining room, just threw me out onto the floor. No training at all. Feeling my way around, I overheard rumors about an affair between the director and assistant director of food and beverage, and I knew this wasn't where I belonged.

While senior leadership was "allegedly" creeping in and out of vacant rooms, I hurt my back trying to overcompensate on the job.

It put me out of work for a while, then as soon as I returned, I was called into a meeting with eight stone-faced members of upper management who scared the hell out of me. They weren't happy about my getting hurt and tried to intimidate me out of my job. I didn't quit on the spot, so they moved me into the, also untrained, role of room service manager. It was a fancy title for being the guy who walked the halls picking up dirty trays and dishes people left outside their doors.

The culture was terrible. Everybody hated their jobs. Manager complaints became employee excuses, and nobody ever got shit done. I can't say I remember what the final straw was, but I do remember what called me away. The job sucked, and one day, I went out with a bunch of guys I had rowed with in college who were in town for an alumni reunion. They were going to watch the Northeastern University men's crew team race down the Charles River, a competition that happened to finish right outside of my hotel. I decided that if I was going to quit, doing so to watch the race with old friends was as good a time as ever.

Operating with Clear Intentions

When you're running your business, it's important to remember: it's not what you do—it's *why* you're doing it. You can't know where you're going without first understanding where you've already come from. As you're picking your way through life's buffet, don't just skip over those memories that leave a sour taste in your mouth. You can experience sweet peace and understanding by taking a nice hearty bite out of not-so-

> As you're picking your way through life's buffet, don't just skip over those memories that leave a sour taste in your mouth.

savory learning lessons.

Company culture is what this is all about. Clipboard systems are easy—that's just math and counting. Nothing new. As I mentioned earlier, the hardest part about this business is getting people to use the systems daily.

It starts with great leadership, and to be clear, being a restaurant owner doesn't immediately qualify you for the job. In this chapter, I'll push you to check yourself and your management to make sure you're trusting the success of your business to the right people. To do that, you'll need to do two things:

- change your company culture and

- create solid core values.

Crazy like a Restaurateur

Before we discuss all the BS that comes with the territory and what you need to do to smooth out the creases in your operations, let's be clear on one thing:

Nowhere in this book will you find some magic trick or super-secret knowledge that'll get you out of hot water. With every system and strategy I share, there's a lot of work to follow.

I can't sell you a glossed-over story of unchallenged success. Being a restaurateur is *hard*. This shit can drive you crazy—if you don't know how to manage the stress.

It's more than mentally draining; it'll break you down physically, too, just like it did with me at the hotel. That was an ugly experience, to say the least. Eventually, things really started to get to me, and I decided I'd had enough: a prime example of how cracks in the company culture can force a business to lose out on people with a lot to offer.

Don't do that. Don't lose out on good talent because you can't get your people under control. Don't risk injuries and workers' comp lawsuits because you don't find the time to properly train and teach everybody what's required of their roles.

The industry is hard, but it can be so simple. Just wait until we break down core values in the next chapter.

Famous Sam's: The First Round Is on Me

What Coyote Springs taught me about culture paid off when I started working with Famous Sam's. Leaving behind my role as operations manager at Coyote Springs, I walked in the door of Famous Sam's as the director of operations! Can you believe it?

That was a major jump for me. From two locations to more than thirty. From manager to having total operations control. I loved the company culture at Coyote Springs at first, but it takes all three gears, which I'll explain in chapter 6, for a restaurant to be successful. For now, Famous Sam's looked like a much more promising picture than some of those dump truck cultures I had worked in before making this career move. In many ways, I could tell that Famous Sam's was going to offer me something I hadn't experienced before. The business was bought by some guys who wanted to take the company public. They gave me the free will to handpick a brand-new operations team and pilot the opening of eight new locations. Like every other position I've held, I went all in as the director. Famous Sam's was going gangbusters with its growth, and I was committed to making it the most profitable, *pleasurable* experience ever.

I used my skill set to create a new franchisee training program from scratch. I was right there, on the ground, opening store after store. I saw what that process was like. I took notes. I soaked it all in, always thinking about what I could gain from each experience. It didn't take long for me to process what happens when you take someone with zero restaurant experience, give them a dynamite system, then back it up with training and support. Famous Sam's taught me the second most important component of success; after culture, you need the numbers to back up all your plans.

Even with the success we saw, I picked up on a few challenges too. Like I said before, there's no getting around the hard work. Back then, there were people who'd been a part of the Famous Sam's system for so long that they had lost the desire to advance. Things were "good enough" for them. But what the hell does that even mean?

Good enough? For whom? For how long? "Good enough" is something my mind still struggles to process because I've always strived to be better. Famous Sam's didn't have the core values in place to keep everyone in line. Without them, people thought they could keep going along with the program.

Like Einstein said, insanity is best described as doing the same thing over and over again yet expecting a different result. If you're crossing your fingers hoping things will get better, you're wasting your time. If you want change to happen, you have to get up and do something about it.

At first, Famous Sam's was on a roll. The trainings I created were provided to franchise owners, which

> If you want change to happen, you have to get up and do something about it.

was a stark contrast to the independents I had worked with before. We were opening stores left and right. I learned how to politic with franchisees and convince people to see the benefits of change and being proactive. I was so committed to being the best in my role that

I was blindsided when I got the news. It only took a year for the guys who bought the business to damn near bankrupt the entire company. Un-freaking-believable.

Upper management jumped ship. Minority shareholders had to step in and bail the business out. By this point, our company culture was a joke, and I knew it wasn't the place I was supposed to be anymore.

Recognizing My Role as a Teacher

I've always been some type of developer, so to speak. Famous Sam's gave me the opportunity to continue that specialty by making it my job to create systems and processes that made sense for the business. When Famous Sam's tanked, it sent me into a completely different field. I found a new love for the industry when I went to work for Scottsdale Culinary Institute.

I taught management and human resources and wines and spirits at Scottsdale. My students learned everything from operations management to French, Italian, German, and California wines. I put together a curriculum to teach them how to use the systems I had developed at Coyote Springs and the trainings I had created for Famous Sam's. Overall, Scottsdale Culinary Institute taught me the power of being proactive. I was able to show my students the right way to manage a restaurant long before they made the same mistakes many owners do every single day. They weren't crossing their fingers hoping textbook examples would come to life. I taught them *exactly* what I taught the franchises. I showed them how to use the benefits of the same systems and tools the major chains used. I proved the need to incorporate a clear, concise operational style along with the power of a positive company culture. I shook things up and shifted everything they thought they knew. And I had a lot of fun doing it.

Always Keep Your Options Open

While I was at the Culinary Institute, my schedule shifted to night courses. But I had a baby on the way, and being a dad trumped everything else. Plus, the politics that come with working in education were driving me nuts, so once again, my game plan needed a few adjustments.

Throughout my career, I've noticed a recurring theme; never keep all your eggs in one basket. I guess I inherited my mom's creativity and drive, so staying stationary was never an option. I knew I had a lot to offer the world. I knew my ideas could really help people feel more fulfilled. Teaching felt great, but I knew there were people who needed my help right now, people who needed guidance to save their businesses. That's when I decided to back up my teaching career with a few professional consulting agreements.

While I was still teaching, would you believe that some of my clients were the same Famous Sam's franchisees I used to work with? When the franchisor fell off, minority shareholders became the majority, and the new owners were begging me to come pitch in.

"David, come back and help us turn the company around and sell it." That was all I ever heard. But as much as I sympathized with their issues, I couldn't take them up on the offer. Consulting was the limit of what I was willing to invest at that point. The company culture I walked away from had left a sour taste in my mouth—I didn't want to deal with that mess for a second round.

Still, the connections remained. My reputation never faded away. The requests kept raining in, and finally, about a month before I had my first child, I said OK.

I came back as the chief operating officer of the thirty-unit franchise chain. I didn't have a full operations team anymore. This time, I had a director of operations working under me. Staff was trimmed down, but there was plenty that needed to be done. Not to mention the stress of getting the company's finances back in order. I'm not one to back down from a challenge, so I agreed to turn the business around in five years.

I don't know if I was crazy or just ridiculously ambitious. To tell you the truth, Famous Sam's should've been bankrupt long before I got there. Everywhere I turned, there was someone else waiting with their hand out. I ended up having to fly out to our bank in California to sort things out.

Thanks to a fast amortization schedule, I created cash flow reports that helped us get a grip on our daily payments and expenses. My systems helped us pinpoint whether we were getting paid franchise fees as scheduled, what outstanding balances needed to be settled, and so much more. Prior to this, this stuff was not being tracked at all!

It was hard. To be honest, it would've been near impossible without my system and my team. That's where company culture comes into play again. People and numbers. You can never get away from them. Not only did we bring things back into balance, we also concentrated on expansion.

We had to turn around backward franchises and open more stores. Five years isn't a long time when you really think about it, but I delivered on my word. Well, it was actually five years and three months, but I don't think they were too concerned.

Million-Dollar Speaking

While I was investing sweat equity into reviving Famous Sam's, my mom came across a seminar called "Million Dollar Speaking." The ticket cost her a hundred bucks, and she was lured in to listen to some guy speak about the business of speaking—not for appearance fees but selling a product on stage and getting your audience to believe in it.

Becoming a professional speaker was never on my radar, but this really intrigued my mom. She went to the seminar and came back raving about how awesome it was. So awesome that she'd already purchased tickets to the next event, and she asked me to tag along.

Naturally, I had a few questions for her. Who was speaking? What were they talking about? Her answers sort of piqued my interest because in college I had majored in speech communications with a focus in interpersonal/organizational communications. I even thought I was going into a career in TV or radio once. Either that or becoming an actor. Then, of course, there was my bid with improv. I don't have stage fright, that's for sure; but professional speaking was different territory.

Still, it wasn't completely unfamiliar. My dad was a neuro-linguistic programming speaker, something like Tony Robbins. He was in the National Speakers Bureau and everything. I mean, seeing him on stage was always so fascinating, so I thought this may not be so bad to see after all. Then I asked a question I immediately regretted. "How much did you pay for it, Mom?"

Four thousand dollars. My mom paid these people a $4,000 up-front investment with $25,000 due on the back end. I went apeshit as soon she said it!

She defended her decision, even backing it up by telling me that they "allow" her to bring somebody for free. (I mean, that's the least they could do after a four-grand commitment!)

The event was in Las Vegas over a four-day stretch. I was sitting there, struggling to focus, and a single question kept circling around in my head: *Is there a manual?*

I interrogated my mother. If there was a manual, nobody had seen it. This time around, I didn't really care that I was being a bitch of a kid because I had to protect my mom. Somebody had just taken advantage of her, and they had to pay for what they'd done.

Going through the motions, I completed day one of the seminar, and I have to say, everything made so much sense. I was still pissed about the money she spent, but that seminar opened my eyes to exactly what I wanted to do and how it had to be done. That's when I accepted my mission to help independents learn how to use the systems and tools the chains use—systems that would change the face of their operations without taking their independence away from them. Systems won't change the fact that you love your guests and your employees, but they do prove that you're ready to start making money like the chains too.

Growing into Your Purpose

By this time, I had been back with Famous Sam's for three years. I went back and explained my game plan to the owners. They wouldn't

> You don't go into business; you grow into business.

try to talk me out of going into business for myself as long as I stayed committed to our agreement.

That's how I got into every single one of my careers. I grew into them. The conscious decisions I thought I was making, like those about comedy and acting, didn't take off like the business I was born into. I needed to be at that conference so I could see exactly why I had experienced all the things I did.

I created my first product shortly after we returned from Vegas. My first two workshops, each four days long, were scheduled while I still sat as chief operating officer at Famous Sam's. Between handling my corporate duties, I traveled the country speaking at events here and there. My start was slow and steady, but I recognized that the real point of everything I was doing wasn't rapid growth; the things I went through showed me how to have the courage to step into new territory.

Smile Button Enterprises, LLC, doing business as TheRestaurantExpert.com, was born in July 2003. I had two desks arranged in the master bedroom of my home and the most motivation I've ever had in my life.

None of this was easy. My first workshop had to be canceled, but that didn't deter me one bit. The first time I spoke to a group, I only had eighteen people's undivided attention. With consistency, and the authenticity of my message, my business grew organically. I never had to force anything.

I didn't have a partner. I didn't have employees. Hell, I didn't even have an office or the first piece of software. I share my story so you can see that it doesn't take a magic pill to make things happen. You just have to be willing to put in the work—and never back down from a challenge.

Over the course of more than a decade, intimate workshop sessions evolved into seminars, trainings, and one-on-one coaching sessions and consultations. I was invited to speak in front of audiences all over the place. I don't just travel to share a story of hope and possibility. I don't spend lots of time bragging about my accomplishments. When I step on stage, it's with one goal in mind: to teach my audience how to make more money.

Unlike that ridiculously overpriced seminar my mother got sucked into, I take pride in delivering an affordable solution to restaurant owners who realize there's a better way to keep their business running. Why join my network? Why listen to anything I have to say? What makes me different from all the rest?

Number one, I don't play games, and I don't have time for bullshit. Number two, I won't blow smoke up your ass by promising things that I haven't tried, tested, and applied time and again. And last but not least, I won't set you up to take on a challenge that's too much for you. I don't just tell you what to do. I show you *how* to do it.

CHAPTER TAKEAWAYS

- Define your "why"—everything else will fall into place.

- Keep your options open; if it doesn't feel good, don't do it!

- Step into your purpose with confidence because someone out there needs you to be successful.

CHAPTER 3

CHANGING CULTURES: THE ROAD TO HIGHER PROFITS AND MORE FREEDOM

Managing people isn't easy. It doesn't matter if you're the overseer for a single restaurant or managing multiple locations, handling a few team members behind the bar or the chef keeping the kitchen in line, you have to juggle a lot at once.

Managing those responsible for managing *others* is an even greater challenge. I've held the role of manager lots of times. I still have to be mindful of certain habits when working with the amazing team I have today, to be honest. In this chapter, we'll begin the long, hard process of chipping away at your company culture to make room for some much-needed change.

Reconstructing Destructed Company Culture

Across the country, independent restaurants suffer because the company culture sucks. It's not always because your people are idiots and don't have an ounce of common sense. Sometimes, poor leadership is to blame for your most expensive problems.

To be clear, we aren't in the food business. If you're worried about coming out as top dog in the food industry, then I can't help you. That's not my area of expertise.

Any restaurant owner who thinks their business is only about food is setting themselves up for failure. If you're competing in the food industry, then you may as well compare yourself to your local gas station. Anyone can get food there, can't they?

What we do is much deeper than food. It relies on training and processes.

When the Hyatt Regency in Cambridge ran me away right after I graduated from college, I gave up on the industry for a bit. Piss-poor leadership and chaos in the business pushed me away from my passion. That's why I had a brief stint as a salesperson for a franchisor for HVAC, plumbing, and electrical franchises that I don't even mention on my résumé. I never saw myself selling HVAC franchises, but it was as far away from hospitality as I could get. Surprisingly enough, things weren't too much better on that side of the spectrum.

Turning your back on your problems won't solve them. I know the restaurant industry has its fair share of kinks, but don't think you'll feel any better by giving up on your dream. Back then, I didn't care. I was young and hopeful, and I didn't have nearly as much invested in the business as you do today. I didn't have half as much experience as I do now either.

The only thing I was focused on was doing something—*anything*—besides food and beverage. Well, about two years later, the company downsized, and I was out of a job again. In desperate need of cash, I went back to what I knew.

I started bartending on the side when I began the franchise sales and compliance consulting business, and that led me to a restaurant that *almost* had the culture side of things figured out. That's what landed me at the Coyote Springs Brewing Company and Café.

Chance and Circumstance Create Opportunity

No matter how far my business expands, I'll always attribute some of my greatest lessons learned to my time at Coyote Springs. Most of the company culture that kept us uplifted and inspired came naturally just from having great people around who knew their jobs and didn't have a problem doing them. Even so, we didn't have the systems we needed to thrive, and we lacked in core values, which left me to figure out the hardest parts of the business by myself.

We needed processes: something tangible and finite that would make the restaurant a better place for the Garrards, the staff, the vendors, and our guests. I managed to make things work, but that didn't mean I escaped unscathed.

I remember one Sunday when we only pulled in $700 for the day. Just $700 in total sales. That was back when I was still behind the bar. After I became a manager, I was able to build sales on Sundays to more than $7,000, and that was only the beginning of our journey.

Success presented some challenges within itself. We started doing so well at the main location that Bill went off to scout location number two. This meant he was gone more often, and in his absence, the restaurant was left with an unexplainable void. That's when our company culture first started to suffer.

> In hindsight, this experience proved that restaurants that depend on the owner's constant, daily presence can't call themselves a successful establishment.

In hindsight, this experience proved that restaurants that depend on the owner's constant, daily presence can't call themselves a successful establishment. Somewhere out there, there's a guy who just read that and said, "OK, fine. I don't need a coach. I'll just hire somebody so I don't have to come in as much." To him, I'd say, you have it all wrong.

I was the employee who was arbitrarily promoted out of the blue. I was the guy who was suddenly dropped into a brand-new position, and to be quite frank with you, it didn't do anything to solve the problem with the restaurant's culture. Transition wasn't easy, but the systems I created help lessen the confusion caused by the shift.

I don't care if you're just breaking into the business or if you've been open for twenty or thirty years; we all experience that one magic restaurant. That one dream team. Coyote Springs was it for me. I worked with a group of people who respected how important we were as a whole. We were all on the same page, so it was a lot easier for me to build a new culture from scratch. This time I was focused on learning from the past.

Think about it for a second—all of this was taking place in the early nineties, when brewpubs were popping up like the plague. Once a week, we'd hear about this new spot and that new place, but that never stopped us from expanding.

That magical staff worked so well that location 2 eventually spread into talks of location 3. Bill placed one of our managers downtown, and I shifted back and forth between both spaces keeping everything (and everyone) up to speed.

In hindsight, I see why Bill wouldn't accept the resignation I offered him about a year into my first management position with Coyote Springs. I was clashing with the GM and thought I would follow my dream to act and do improv as a career choice. Since he wouldn't let me quit, I ended up manning my role as operations manager for two more years. Back then, I may have been a little reluctant about sticking around, but today I am so glad I did. The lessons I learned over those next few years helped place so many other things into perspective for me. I guess I needed some more time to learn from my environment, more time to perfect the things I needed to know to be able to provide independent restaurant owners with chain-worthy systems.

Thinking on Your Feet

Successful owners know how to be adaptable. A good independent knows that it's their job to stay on top of any new projects or creative developments; they aren't afraid to keep their eyes facing forward, building their business with the future in mind. My experience at Coyote Springs also taught me another valuable lesson, one I hope you hold on to while you implement the changes you learn in this book.

Timing is everything. Coyote Springs opened up that second location in downtown Phoenix years before the area took off. The Phoenix Coyotes, Arizona's NHL team, had just gotten into the arena, which eventually brought us a little growth. Still, I think we pulled trigger on that location just a little too soon. Sure, we knew all about the plans to expand and build hotels in that area, but they weren't even built yet. There was a lot of future potential for that area, and I can see why Bill would want to be one of the first restaurants around, but nobody had a reason to go downtown back then. That killed the location for us.

It was a struggle, but when the chips are down, I never get up from the table. We made that situation work for the greater good of the restaurant, and I worked on mastering my poker face as I was hit with another unexpected blow. One day, Bill spoke to me about another surprise assignment. He took me away from my management role to work on a two-week-long budget project. To some, that may not seem like a long time, but imagine what it would be like if one of your managers went on vacation for two weeks and you still have shifts to run. Now think about what it was like for two restaurants!

Bill said he put me on the budget because it was "proactive." Right then and there I learned that true success can only be measured by one's commitment to progress. You have to keep pushing, you have to keep learning, you have to keep raising your standards.

> Experience holds no value if it can't be transferred.

Coming out from behind the bar taught me that I had the ability to manage $3.5 million in sales annually. I could manage entire management teams while wrangling and training over one hundred employees. My vision, my experience, and my tenacity helped me develop operational SMART systems that changed the way my restaurants serviced the world.

My systems make complicated processes simple, measurable, applicable, repeatable, and, most importantly, trainable. I share a lot of tips throughout this book, so much that I'm sure some sections may require a few extra reads, but I'll do you a favor and spare you some time by sharing one of my best secrets right now: keep it simple.

The key with any system is that it has to be simple, or nobody will use it. Likewise, if it's not trainable, it'll be virtually impossible for you to show your team how to put it to use.

> The harder things get, the more you can expect to learn from them.

Hard-Knock Lessons

Those days of learning how to manage and operate restaurants put me through some of the most unbelievably difficult trials I've ever endured, but I learned something from every single one of them. I was lucky enough to have an all-access pass to someone else's problems. I learned from mistakes without suffering direct consequences. I did my best to assume someone else's risks and responsibilities, and it stressed the hell out of me, but I got to see what happens when things go wrong before they went wrong for me. I got to witness the impact of negative cash flow. I learned what it was like to have to manage people of different skill sets and backgrounds and beliefs. Even with all the systems and instructions in the world, there's nothing that can quite compare to real-world, on-the-job training.

Those experiences also helped me witness the unspoken detriment of success. Everybody wants to succeed, right? Every company's mission statement and core value agreement probably include some mention of success. Most people consider success to be an achievement, but few discuss what can happen when a business isn't ready to succeed.

Growth is a good thing when the business is prepared to manage the expansion. When you spread your wings too far, too soon, though, you start to unravel all the good that made your restaurant desirable from the start.

I sat and watched as we lost good people, something else a textbook or pep talk never could've prepared me for. Because of the negative cash flow, which created negative attitudes, we had to fire four managers in two locations on the same day. That wasn't an easy recovery for the restaurant, and our culture suffered as well. We lost our magic. Growth had tipped the scales, and Coyote Springs wasn't prepared to restore the balance. Looking back years later, I realized that we were struggling to get over something that the systems I'm offering today could've helped us avoid.

Accountability Begins at the Head of the Table

How many times have you found yourself completely pissed off—ready to blow your lid—because of something your managers did?

How many times have you closed your eyes and envisioned wringing someone's neck for making a mistake that could've been avoided with common sense?

You can yell, scream, and shout all you want, but that won't change a thing. At the end of the day, you're responsible for any and every decision your team makes.

If somebody drops the ball, you have to take responsibility for the fumble. If you're convinced that you've staffed a bunch of idiots, think about the fact that you're the one who picked them.

You hired them. You trained them. You manage them every day. If they're idiots, they're your idiots, and you created them, so what are you going to do about it?

The only solution you can count on is laying out the systems your restaurant needs to increase your profits and productivity, training your people to navigate those systems, and then holding them to the process. Accountability is the game changer that'll keep your business out of the red.

> Good people can't be found; they are created.

The Dream Equation

Once the system is in place, the gray area ceases to exist. I follow what I like to call the "dream equation": your **Dream = Core Values + Purpose + Mission.**

You can't keep hiring chain managers and hoping they fix your problems straight out of the gate. Always remember, it doesn't matter how much success someone's seen at another company; the only way they'll be able to succeed in your business is if you give them the tools to do it.

> Core values are the foundation for the development of good people and great leaders.

Creating Core Values

Start changing the way you think right now. No part of your dream should include you, the owner, slaving away on the clock. You don't have to be the chef. You don't need to work the line. You don't need to drive yourself crazy just to keep your business on track. All you need to do is execute your dream equation.

The time you spend washing dishes in your own business is time taken away from interacting with your guests. That's the best way to kill the customer experience and shatter the message your restaurant sends to the world. Restaurateurs cannot afford to waste any time on anything that doesn't directly grow their business. Once they realize how important it is to make sure that all three components of the dream equation align, every owner who goes through my coaching program has a serious epiphany. They realize that it's time to put down the scrubbers and scrapers and pick up a few systems that'll keep their restaurants running up to their standards, even if they aren't around. The first step in making this transition is tightening up your restaurant's core values.

Core values are who you are as a person; they almost never change. They become your guiding principles for running your restaurant. They are the compass your management team uses to make decisions in your stead.

A couple of years back, I hosted a seminar called "Restaurant Accountability." It was a total hit! Everyone grabbed ahold of that message and took off running. I knew "Restaurant Accountability" had the potential to open quite a few independent owners' eyes but seeing that response proved to me that someone needs to put some steam behind this message. It showed me how important it was for people to understand that accountability through core values was another major key the industry was missing. Married to the need to make a difference, to enlighten the very restaurateurs who struggle like my mom used to in our family's restaurant, that "someone" quickly became me.

I decided to start this accountability revolution by making sure restaurant owners clearly understood what core values represent. First, you have to understand that your core values exist deep inside of you—they aren't something you can create.

That's how you know they're authentic.

When we ask owners to write their core values, they aren't pulling them out of thin air; they're simply documenting the triggers that already exist within them. Core values are verbs. They're what you *do*, not what you say. I see a lot of businesses that get wrapped up in drafting these long, drawn-out core value announcements, and they never follow through with the damn thing. This part of the dream equation isn't about talking a good game. Just focus on documenting the things you've always believed in.

Core values need to be clear and concrete. They need to be written down and displayed somewhere that makes them easy to see. Intertwine your core values with your restaurant's culture. Make them the topic of conversation. Core values are motivators, drivers that encourage your employees to create an unforgettable experience for your guests. They should be drilled into your staff's heads from open to close every day.

How do you do that? By recognizing what makes core values so important.

When used properly, these agreements will break the chain that keeps you tied to your restaurant 365 days a year. They give you the freedom to venture off to the four corners of the globe without ever thinking twice about what's happening at your business. Core values make you confident in your management team's ability to keep things moving in your absence.

Beyond your vision and mission statement, core values set the tone for your employees, your vendors, and your guests. They tell everyone what they can expect every single time they visit your establishment.

Let's use these as an example:

Excellence. We strive to achieve and maintain excellence in everything we do. To us, excellence is measured one happy guest at a time. We earn the loyalty of our guests by our commitment to making them our main priority. We empower and encourage every team member to do whatever it takes to make our guests happy. Knowing they have the full support of the entire company behind them enables team members to deliver on our commitment to excellence.

Hospitality. A great hospitality experience is when guests can focus on each other and have a good time. It's creating an environment where relationships are celebrated, where people can laugh, talk, enjoy great food and drinks together, and let their guards down. We want our guests to choose to visit us because we've created a strong personal connection and they feel like we are their home away from home.

Quality. From the very beginning, quality at all levels of our operation has been a driving force behind our success. We use systems to ensure our quality standards are met. This starts with making sure we execute on the basics first, which include clean and safe work environments, hot food hot, cold food cold, great food, and great service. And then we move on to creating a culture in our restaurant where we have pride in the food and beverage we serve, our plate presentations, and the businesses we run. By maintaining high quality standards, we ensure our guests keep coming back.

Consistency. We believe consistency is key to a great dining experience. We want our guests to know exactly what to expect each and every time they dine with us. To ensure consistency in our products and service, we will follow operational systems for everything from food quality and preparation to caring customer service and cleanliness.

Integrity. We will act with unwavering integrity with every action we take. To us, integrity is doing what we know is right even when it is not expected and especially when it may be hard. While we understand nobody is perfect, we will hold ourselves accountable when we falter and will do everything in our power to make things right.

Learning. With our core values as a guide and our ambition to always be looking for ways to improve every aspect of our business, from service to menu, operational systems to training, and efficiencies to cleanliness, we are committed to continual learning and personal growth. We will facilitate this journey as a company by creating a positive work environment where continual learning is the norm by providing ongoing training and positive feedback and by always being open to change.

It isn't hard to tell how your core values can double as a snapshot employee manual, especially when you can see them written down on paper. Reading them aloud to your staff is like a constant reminder of how the core values you've chosen represent the guiding principles that outline how you want your restaurant run, whether you are present or not.

> Your core values must be personal. That's how you put, and keep, the passion in your business.

Your core values must be personal. That's how you put, and keep, the passion in your business. Don't worry about what you think they should sound like, just concentrate on trying to remain as authentic and transparent as you can.

It's one thing to sit down and say, "I'll write out some core values." It's another to know how to put those values into action.

These statements are more than a feel-good declaration, they're a solid reminder of how you want your business to run. It's how you want to be remembered at the end of each day. Some owners planned to create something to pass down to family. Others were interested in serving the community. You could've jumped into this business just to make big bucks. Whatever your main focus, it needs to be translated into your core values.

Creating Your Core Values

Your core values can be a single word, a sentence, or a few paragraphs. The following is an exercise that I use to help owners write out core values that really matter to them. It's a five-step process that'll change every decision made on behalf of your business.

Step 1. Look through the list of core value words (check the resources section at the end of the book), and place a check mark next to every word that calls to you, whatever you identify with either personally or professionally.

Step 2. Review the words you've chosen, and eliminate any with redundant meanings.

Step 3a. If there's only one owner, do the following:

- Transfer your list to a blank sheet of lined paper.

- Cross off any words that don't call to you anymore.

- Put a star (*) beside the words that really hit you in the gut.

- Place a question mark (?) next to the words you like but that may still be redundant. (You may be able to work these into your core value descriptions.)

Step 3b. If you're working with a partner, family member, or spouse, it's time to compare your lists for similarities. Somebody take the lead and grab a second sheet of paper.

- Read a word from your list, then ask your partner if they have one like it. For example, *honesty* and *integrity* are pretty close.

- Write similar word pairs on one line, for example, honesty/integrity.

- Repeat these steps until you've listed all the word pairs from your lists.

Step 4. Decide which of the word pairs on each line match both of your expectations, and pick one to become a potential core value. (Note: don't think about the customers—think about who you are and how you want your business to operate.)

Step 5. Start writing!

One of my good friends, who was a member and a coach at my previous company, David Millitello, spoke at one of our seminars and said, "You're gonna know what your core values are because it's when you get pissed off in your business because one of your team members stepped on your core values."

> Core values must be something visceral; you feel it in your gut. It's who you are as a person.

What grinds your gears? Pinpoint that trigger, and start building your core values from there.

In chapter 4, I'll share a way for you to guarantee that every time your managers make a decision based on *your* core values, not their own, they'll make the right move. With this one system, your managers won't ever get in trouble again. Instead, you'll learn how to transform a breach in your core values into a coaching opportunity.

CHAPTER TAKEAWAYS

Remember the dream equation: Dream = Core Values + Purpose + Mission.

- Core values are supported by the things you do, not what you say.

- **Free download:** Core Values Special Report. https://www.davidscottpeters.com/book-bonuses

CHAPTER 4

SUCCESS IS A BASIC CONCEPT; DON'T OVERCOMPLICATE IT

Simplicity makes it easier for people to stick to the program. Before we get into more complicated management responsibilities like calculating your dollars per labor hour, ask yourself, Am I taking care of the basics in my restaurant?

In my family, I'm the risky, out-of-his-mind entrepreneur. My wife, not so much. She's more of the practical one who prefers security over chance and thrill. I'm the antithesis that's always pushing for change and adventure. It could create conflict in our relationship if we let our own points of focus and interests take precedent, but we respect our common ground and keep things simple.

These "opposites attract" business partnerships can keep things interesting in your business, but they don't need to lead to earth-shattering disputes. Whether you're teaming up with your spouse or your childhood best friend, your task is to level the playing field in that partnership with a common denominator. Just by writing out a set of shared core values for your restaurant, core values written with input from everyone, not in favor of one partner or the other, you can avoid the costly effects of miscommunication. It's the only way my wife and I get things done as well as we do. Everyone needs to be committed to the core values you attach to your business. If one partner doesn't feel heard, they probably won't be as invested in upholding the standards you want to be known for. That's when everything tends to start rolling downhill.

In my work with restaurant owners, I get all types of inquiries from split-owner independents, especially spouse partnerships. It's not always the simplest task, but if my wife can continue to tolerate my random adventures, then I think there's still hope for you and your partner(s). To give you an idea of how things are done, let's look at how I worked with two husband-and-wife duos to create core values that made sense for both partners.

First, I'll use a couple I coached in the past, the owners of Nero's Restaurant, as an example. Their core values are

- family,

- integrity,

- teamwork,

- training, and

- hospitality.

We'll compare them to another owner, of the Dunes Restaurant, who has core values including

- family,

- tradition,

- excellence,

- accountability,

- consistency, and

- hospitality.

Now, how do these two groups of values compare? We can see that both couples hold family as a core value, but the word means something different to each of them. Since the words and phrases we use can be interpreted in many different ways, it's important to clearly define the meaning behind the core values you select for your business.

With Nero's, *family* means the following: "Our deep faith and belief in the Golden Rule guides us to treat everyone with care and respect. Our goal is to be a role model in our community and our restaurant. We love both our guests and staff and feel that they are all a part of our extended family."

Their definition of family carries more of a religious undertone. Nero's wishes to uphold the Golden Rule and treat others how they wanted to be treated in return.

In contrast, the Dunes Restaurant provides this definition for *family*: "The Dunes Restaurants opened their doors in 1979. A few years later, Roxy and Rufus Pritchard followed their dream of running their own family business and purchased the restaurant in 1983. The restaurant is currently run by two generations of Pritchards alongside their employees whom they think of as extended family, as many of them have been at the Dunes for more than twenty years. To us, family is the most important thing in the world. Therefore, we strive to keep our Dunes family happy and protect their well-being while within these walls. We operate on this level to ensure our restaurant family can also provide for their own families."

To them, it's less about external connections and more about their family, in a literal and figurative sense. Their staff is made up of relatives and employees they consider family, so they strive to protect and take care of everyone like blood. The Dunes Restaurant recognizes that life outside of the business is out of their control, but as long as their family is inside the building, they'll do whatever to make sure they're provided for.

You can ask ten people to define the core value vocabulary words you've chosen and you'll probably walk away with ten different explanations. The way I approach developing core values brings simplicity back into the equation. That way there's less room for error.

Make It Work for Your Business

Using *your* restaurant's core values as a guide, your managers can make the right decisions when faced with any problem. They may not always get it right the first time around, but that just presents an opportunity for more coaching.

> Shit should only hit the fan in your restaurant when your managers directly go against the core values you've outlined for them.

You have to have some faith in your people before you write them off for good. If you do your part as the restaurant's owner and provide your employees with the systems and tools they need to do their jobs correctly, you'll find less and less reason to flip your lid. Shit should only hit the fan in your restaurant when your managers directly go against the core values you've outlined for them. Luckily, that shouldn't be happening anyway. If you keep things simple and take advantage of every coaching opportunity you see, applying your core values to daily business decisions should be easy.

Here are two examples to help prove my point. The first is about a manager who makes a decision that isn't congruent with the restaurant's core values, and the other shows what can happen when a manager uses your core values to make a good decision, even if it isn't perfect. Here's the core value we want to focus on right now:

Excellence. We believe that it is not only our job but our responsibility. Our job is to ensure we are the best! We do this by only buying the best ingredients and hiring and training only the best. We strive for 100 percent guest satisfaction. Our success in achieving excellence is measured one happy customer at a time.

You've trained and coached your managers on the importance of excellence, and it's clear that it's a responsibility you expect them to uphold. With this understood, one day, your manager discovers that you're short on the steaks you need for an upcoming party. They know there won't be enough time to get steaks hotshot delivered. So your manager decides to run to the grocery store instead. While standing at the butcher counter, the manager makes a decision based on what your core values mean to them.

SCENARIO 1—BAD CHOICE

The manager purchases the cheapest steaks they can find. These steaks are very low quality. Later that night, you stop in to check on the party only to discover that the steaks coming out of the kitchen are garbage! Immediately, you're embarrassed and pissed off.

You approach the manager and ask: "How did you decide on these steaks?" When the manager replies, "I just figured the cheaper the better to save money," you blow a gasket because the quality is light-years away from your core value.

SCENARIO 2—BETTER CHOICE

The manager purchases the most expensive steaks they can find. In fact, they are a much higher quality than the customer requested. The price per pound is almost double what was expected on the recipe costing card.

Later that night, you stop in to check on the party and hear about how you were shorted on the steak delivery. You ask the manager, "How much did these steaks cost?" After hearing the total, you start to feel yourself getting upset. Then you ask, "How did you decide on these steaks?"

The manager replies, "Based on our core value of excellence, I made sure we purchased only the best the store had to offer. I wanted to make sure everyone was 100 percent happy with their meal."

The decision was made based on your core values, so how can you be mad? Don't punish the manager; instead, coach them on how you would have gone about making the decision yourself.

Dan Carr, an owner I worked with at my former company, took what we showed him about core values and simplified his life to the tenth power. From that moment forward, whenever an employee came to him with a question or a problem, he'd simply reply, "How does that fit with our core values?"

It's that easy, guys!

The Restaurant Prosperity Formula™

Restaurant 101 is all about the basics. It's the core of who we are and what we do in this business. It starts with hospitality. Before any of my systems can work for you, you have to know how to offer your guests a mind-blowing, out-of-this-world experience. They need *wow* customer service! Hot food has to be hot, and cold food must stay cold. There should be a clean, safe environment for your guests and employees and incredible food and drink. My Restaurant Prosperity Formula explains exactly what you need to do to deliver an incredible product to your guests, something that will keep them coming back.

First, if you don't get the basics of Restaurant 101, nothing else matters. Once you master the preliminary tasks that keep restaurants in business, cash controls and checklists follow because they allow you to create a culture in your restaurant where the details matter. We'll talk more about this in the next chapter.

> You're not ready for change until you understand the basics.

Now, to take your restaurant to the next level, meaning it's making you money, you've given yourself the freedom to leave your restaurant in the competent hands of the strong management team you've trained to operate it, and you're fully aware of what goes into the Restaurant Prosperity Formula.

After teaching, training, and coaching literally thousands upon thousands of restaurant owners and managers over the length of my broad career, I can pinpoint what makes one restaurant owner successful and what turns another one into a failure. The reason usually falls somewhere on a two-point spectrum. The success of your restaurant directly depends on the owner's personality traits and the very specific actions they take on a daily basis.

At my past company, I worked with a diverse group of restaurant owners from all over North America. Every quarter, we met as a group to learn from each other, share ideas, ask for help, and be held accountable. During one of those meetings, I hijacked the discussion and asked twenty-two of our most successful restaurant owners what it was that made them successful. Mind you, the vast majority of the restaurant owners who were sitting at this table had been working with me for an average of ten to twelve years. While I wasn't surprised by what they shared with me, I did use it to help me explain successful restaurant operation in a simple, consistent, easily trainable process.

The first thing I picked up on as we went around the table was that they *all* had two personality traits in common. Every owner in that room was right about one thing: their *passion* and *persistence* helped them overcome the same challenges and disputes that turn less devoted owners off. When it comes to passion, they were all passionate about hospitality, and they used that passion to drive them to do what they had to do to create memories for their guests. This was often one of the main reasons these owners got into the restaurant business. The next trait I identified was an unmatched level of persistence, which was probably the biggest reason they were successful. Coming from different backgrounds, with different goals and different core values, they each said that they would never allow anything in this world to stop them from realizing their dreams.

Every owner in that room understood that challenges are inevitable. They knew that there wasn't anything they could do to permanently avoid the unexpected events that could cost them money, time, and sometimes, their *peace of mind*, but they were not going to let those challenges stop them. Instead, they had resolved to keep their heads down and stay focused on grabbing the brass ring. These are traits that every hopeful restaurateur needs to embody.

The next thing this group taught me was that they all took certain actions every day. The things they did weren't exactly groundbreaking, but I discovered that, if more people who wanted to be successful in the restaurant business would follow their lead, anyone could be successful in this industry. That realization inspired me to place the finishing touches on a new training system, and the Restaurant Prosperity Formula was coined from that mission.

This formula is broken down into five distinct action categories. These categories are leadership, systems, training, accountability, and taking action. The actual formula is prosperity equals leadership plus systems and training over accountability plus taking action. It looks like this:

$$\text{PROSPERITY} = \text{LEADERSHIP} + \frac{\text{SYSTEMS} + \text{TRAINING}}{\text{ACCOUNTABILITY}} + \text{TAKING ACTION}$$

Prosperity is having a thriving, profitable restaurant that gives you the freedom to leave your restaurant because you have a management team that knows their job, how to do it, how well it needs to be done, and by when.

To achieve this level of success (prosperity), you have to be a leader in your business, have systems in place for everything you do, constantly learn and train, hold your management team accountable, and most importantly, take action!

Let's take a deeper look at the different variables in this equation.

Leadership requires a restaurant leader who makes decisions based on the systems and numbers produced by their restaurant, someone capable of leading their team with strong communication skills. The truth of the matter is that simply owning or managing a restaurant doesn't make you a great leader. But it does take strong leadership to be successful. One of the most beautiful parts about the Restaurant Prosperity Formula is the way it allows leaders to naturally take care of their team just by following the other four action categories.

Systems are the implementation of a step-by-step process for everything that needs to be done to run a successful restaurant, no matter how small or large, which allows a restaurant owner or manager to impose their will without being there. This is the exact way chain restaurants are able to expand all over the world. It's because there is a system, a process, a way to doing anything, in fact, *everything*. That system is documented, easily trainable, and managed for efficiency. Chain restaurants leave nothing to chance—or worse to "common" sense. In those restaurants, when any team member does their job, they follow a very carefully laid out process that can be duplicated time after time. Systems are why chains can maintain a consistent customer experience across hundreds or even thousands of restaurants.

> This is the exact way chain restaurants are able to expand all over the world. It's because there is a system, a process, a way to doing anything, in fact, *everything*.

Training is the ongoing information gathering, education, and instruction of the restaurant's management and team members toward constant restaurant operational and financial improvement. It means you never stop learning, seeking information to improve your restaurant, and never stop sharing with your team, at all levels, based on their levels of authority.

Accountability is something I like to refer to as *answerability* because some people view accountability as a negative word or action.

When we reframe it as answerability, it's easy to understand that as long as you have provided your team the training, systems, and coaching to be successful at their jobs, when they are held accountable for not doing their jobs, you can't be the bad guy and they aren't victims. Instead, they understand how the mistake was their fault because they're able to identify what should've been done using the relevant system for the job. Accountability, or answerability, is the acknowledgment of responsibility for your obligations, decisions, and actions and reminds your employees that they are answerable for the resulting consequences.

Building on that point, let's take a look at what those responsibilities look like for your team:

- Obligations mean performing your job to meet a specific list of expectations.

- Decisions are choices you make based on your obligations. In other words, you get to decide if you're going to do your job.

- Actions are what you do as a result of your decisions, which are ultimately that basis for what you will be accountable/answerable for.

This could be one of the hardest parts of the equation. If you ultimately don't hold people accountable, you will *not* be successful.

Taking action is arguably the most critical part of the formula. To take action is to take responsibility for your success by consciously performing acts that move you toward your goals of running a profitable restaurant and getting your life back. I think it's best summarized by a phrase my dad, Howard Gray Peters, used to use: "Ideas are cheap. It's the people who put them into action that are priceless." This book is going to give you a ton of actionable ideas, but if you don't take action on any of them, you will not get results. And this is something that—to a person—successful restaurant owners do: they take action!

If you use this book as your guide, by the end you will have everything you need to be prosperous. All you have to do is remember that to get results you simply have to start somewhere, anywhere, and take action.

CHAPTER TAKEAWAYS

- Keep it simple by focusing on your core values.
- Remember the Restaurant Prosperity Formula.
- Taking action, day after day, is what restaurant leadership is all about.

CHAPTER 5

CHECKLISTS: THE FORMULA FOR FINANCIAL INDEPENDENCE

Systems provide you with a foolproof opportunity to get out of your own way. Remember, just because you're a restaurant owner doesn't mean you're a born leader. Those who don't have those natural skills have to work twice as hard because no matter what road you travel to get where you're trying to go, it takes leadership to be successful. If you weren't born to lead, it's time to get things into gear. First things first, you need to organize your operation so it can start functioning more efficiently.

The next very important step in establishing consistency in your restaurant is to get everyone on your team to understand what their roles and responsibilities are. If your goal is to create a smooth-running operation, everyone who works for your restaurant—from line employees to partners—must know what everyone else is responsible for. When there's no room for anyone to confuse what their coworkers are supposed to be doing, you'll virtually eliminate any conflict, especially in the complex professional relationship between partners, family members, and management.

· · · · · · · · · · ·

Without the organizational chart, confusion, discord and conflict become the order of the day. But with it, the direction, purpose and style of the business are balanced, interacting purposefully and progressing with intention and integrity toward a cohesive and sensible whole.

—Michael Gerber, The E-Myth Revisited

· · · · · · · · · · ·

I've illustrated this organizational design in the past, using a three-step process inspired by *The E-Myth Revisited* by Michael Gerber. This process outlines what's required to define roles in your organization. It explains the need to do the following:

- Map out your organizational chart for the company you ultimately want to build (not necessarily what you have today).

- Assign job duties to each position.

- Assign the names of all the key people to each of the positions. (Some key people will have their names on multiple positions.)

Gerber insists that the organizational chart should be a part of the initial business plan. In other words, when everyone understands their role in the company, things get done and people aren't so resentful. The tone you set trickles down to your employees, your customers, and your family. That's why nothing should be left to interpretation.

Your checklists and cash controls keep the basics of restaurant operations in check. They're what keep hot food hot and cold food cold. They maintain a clean, safe work environment. They deliver the *wow* customer service experiences your guests are looking for. They create incredible products that live up to your core values. Checklists and cash controls are the glue that holds your restaurant together—they help us do what we've been put on earth to do.

> Profitability doesn't matter if your restaurant sucks. Checklists and cash controls help maintain your standards.

We're in the hospitality industry. We create memories for our guests. When someone dines in your restaurant and has a mind-blowing experience, they expect the same thing every time they come back. Profitability doesn't matter if your restaurant sucks. Checklists and cash controls help maintain your standards.

You need them to create a culture in the business where the details matter. If I can't get a manager to follow a checklist, if I can't get a dishwasher or any line employee to follow a checklist and do the basics, what makes you think I can get a manager to wake up bright and early on a Sunday morning excited to take inventory that evening—and do it accurately?

I can't.

And if that's the case, there's no way I can keep up with Restaurant 101.

Simplistic Innovation

When I created my first ordering system at Coyote Springs, I had to manually transfer it to each location using a modem and pcAnywhere software. Imagine what it was like to drag your system's programming back and forth just to try to keep your data organized.

Yes, it was *that* long ago.

It may have been a pain in the ass, but still, it was amazingly innovative for the times we were in, and it was ten times better than what we had—which was nothing.

Expansion brought plenty of struggle along with it. My skills were really put to the test when Bill, the restaurant's owner, took his family to Ireland to tour the Guinness brewery.

"David, you're gonna pay the bills." That's how I was trained on cash flow management. Then Bill left the country.

It seemed simple enough. Our first location—the magic location—was still a freaking cash cow at that point. Location two, on the other hand, was beginning to show the first signs of it being a money pit—which we all know is a restaurant owner's worst nightmare.

We couldn't enjoy any profits at the first location before the other restaurant sucked it all away like a greedy vampire. In the downtown location, bills piled up twice as fast as the money came in. I couldn't figure out how to manage it. That's where proper training could've saved me.

So many independents think they can run their restaurants from the gut. Instinct is one hell of an asset, but it can also hold you back if you aren't careful. That's why I'm such a strong advocate for systems and processes. I've learned from some pretty expensive mistakes. As I mentioned before, Coyote Springs didn't perform well when Bill was away. So as one would expect, his international vacation threw our operations out of whack. And it all happened for two reasons:

1. The budget was not followed.

2. I was basically thrown the keys and told good luck.

Entrepreneurs usually feel the need to do everything themselves. When you take on as much responsibility as Bill was famously known for, you can almost guarantee that no one else in your restaurant is trained on what needs to be done. This one-man-band style of restaurant management turns your business into your own personal prison, and it stagnates your profitability.

That time when Bill left the country, my worst nightmare was fulfilled. Imagine how it feels to interrupt the boss's vacation and tell him we couldn't make payroll. We solved the problem with a cash call to our investors, but proper cash flow management and following our budget could've eliminated the issue altogether. A restaurant with no systems is bound to end up in total chaos.

Growth Is a Costly Process

Cost is so much more than dollars and cents. Even before you can calculate your returns, think about all the time you've invested into your business. I put eighty-hour weeks into perfecting all my systems. That type of on-the-job training can cost independent restaurant owners more time and money than they can actually afford to lose. Tossing an unqualified, untrained employee into an important role is one of the easiest ways to watch your money go down the drain. They'll be on the clock, on your dime, trying to figure out what to do, and nine times out of ten, they won't be able to guess their way to success, so that'll probably cost you too. Today, I'm proud to offer restaurant owners a solution. After learning from my old friend's mistakes, I'm happy to have the chance to teach independents the systems that streamline processes that used to take us days, if not weeks, to complete.

Untangling the payroll issues at Coyote Springs was one thing, but I learned the real importance of timely profit and loss statements while sifting through boxes of bank and merchant account statements that hadn't been looked at for more than two years.

At some point, Bill decided to fire the firm that did our accounting and taxes. Two years later, he decided I was the man he wanted to handle it instead.

There I was, knee deep in the chaos that was a storm of old reports with a head full of unanswered questions. Imagine my thoughts when I discovered we hadn't filed our 8027 Tip Report with the IRS in more than two years. Next thing you know, we got audited.

We brought in an accounting firm to help us with the books, but there was still two years' worth of reconciliation that had to be done. I literally smacked my head trying to fumble through the basement to find boxes filled with the daily envelopes that held credit card receipts. I discovered $10,000 in missing money from Diners Club. Do you remember Diners Club? Old or not—that's a hell of a lot of missing money.

Once again, systems could've helped us avoid some costly mistakes. One thing I need every restaurant owner out there to understand is you can't be everywhere at once. You can't be the manager, chef, accountant, buyer, supplier, host, and server. You have a staff for a reason. You pay them to do a job for you. It's time to start cleaning up your day-to-day operations. And that's exactly what I'm showing you how to do now.

All systems are checklists. I know I've mentioned this a few times by now, but you should be able to leave your restaurant without fearing that everything will fall apart if you aren't there. It's time to cure yourself of "common sense-itis."[1]

It's not common sense. It's never common sense.

Your managers can't use "common sense" and just do what needs to be done how you expect them to do it. They aren't mind readers.

When we look at the definition of common sense, it clearly states that it's a shared understanding based on experience. I can tell you right now that your managers, each and every one of them, do not share your experiences.

They haven't grown up in your shoes. They haven't seen the same things. Their core values may be completely different from anything you come up with. You aren't the same people, which means they'll never just correctly assume how you want things done simply because you think your way of thinking is common.

Realizing that common sense doesn't exist frees you to quickly accept your responsibility to tell your people exactly what you want done, how to do it, how well you want it done, and by when.

Let's get rid of common sense-itis once and for all. It's costing you a lot of money!

---

1   What is common sense-itis? Everyone's suffered from it at some point in their lives. It's when we get caught up on the working definition of common sense. Based on a strict construction of the term, it consists of what people in the common world would agree on: that which they "sense" as their common natural understanding. The "itis" comes from the Greek language and means "inflammation." So I define common sense-itis as the "never-ending headache you have from repeatedly banging your head against a brick wall when you enter your restaurant." This term is shockingly accurate when you apply it to how most restaurant owners think their managers should do things.

Writing Checklists

To be clear, systems don't matter if you don't have a great restaurant to begin with. If you aren't putting out great food and offering a great experience in a clean space people love to visit—who cares what kind of systems you come up with? They won't matter because your restaurant is already working backward. On the other hand, when you have happy customers and happy employees, we can start making things happen.

Restaurant 101 doesn't mean you're systems ready. That's just rounding first base. With the foundation laid, checklists and cash controls become the next thing you need to focus on. When you walk through your restaurant, you should know exactly where to find whatever you need. Everything is in its proper place. All things are secured according to the checklists you've provided to your employees.

There isn't any random cash in a desk drawer that you use to grab extra change when the bar drawer won't balance. You need to know what your overs and shorts are every night. Your people need to know that more than five dollars over/under per set of hands in the cash drawer can cost them their job. I mean, if they can't count, they have no business working for you.

You need a system in place that allows you to capture every penny the server report says is due from each server. There is no rounding up or down. And then you need a system to know when the daily deposit actually hits the bank.

If your cash controls aren't handled, you need to go back and start retraining your staff on best practices for your restaurants. Once you've gotten that underway, you still won't be ready to start using systems until you get your checklists in order. Listen, I don't want to hear, "checklists don't work." They do. Checklists work so well that they're the foundation of *all* our systems.

I can already hear what you're saying. "Bullshit, man. We got checklists. They suck. They don't work. We've tried them before."

Whenever I hear this, I just throw it right back. I'll look directly at those restaurant owners and their managers and say, "Bullshit. Yes, they do."

Don't tell me that checklists don't work. *Yours* don't work because they suck and you're holding the wrong people accountable for those checklists. Plain and simple. Fortunately, I'm not here to tease you; I'm here to teach you exactly what to do to turn your restaurant around and make it more successful than it's ever been. I've gone the extra mile to get you set up because I know there's only so much I can cover in a book. We're going to walk through what you need to do to start creating checklists that actually work. Then I want you to follow the link in the resources section to https://www.davidscottpeters.com/book-bonuses.

Now that you're ready to give checklists a shot (the *right* way, this time), let's go over what you need to do:

Step 1. Create opening and closing checklists for every shift you run (every single position, managers included).

Step 2. Follow up on the checklists to make sure the process is working and your managers are doing their jobs.

It's simple, right? Just like I promised.

Doing the work is the hardest part, and follow-through comes in as a close second. The reason why most restaurant owners' checklists fail is because they sucked from the moment they were created. Don't tell me it's too hard or it's too much work. I'll tell you like my mom told me—suck it up, buttercup!

You're damn right it's hard. We're in one of the toughest industries anybody could choose. If you're looking to reduce your stress levels, start using checklists as a tool.

Let's get started. Yep, right now! There's no better time than the present. Go grab a pen and paper.

Now stand outside your front door and take a long, deep breath. Once your mind is clear, think about all the things you see every day that piss you off. Before you walk inside the restaurant, survey the parking lot. Look at the grounds around your restaurant.

Do you see litter? Is anything in need of repair?

Walk around to the back. Check out the back. What's going on out there? Are your employees discarding trash like you asked? Is there anything back there that'd embarrass you if your guests saw it?

Remember, no detail is too big or too small.

Next, you're going to walk inside the restaurant and do the same thing. Look at everything. Spacing. Placement. Are the plants in the event room dying of thirst? Is the toilet paper roller broken in the ladies' room? Does the dispenser have soap?

Halfway through this exercise, you're going to feel enraged. As your list of pet peeves starts to pile up, you're going to be pissed! You're going to picture me in your head and say, "Hey! I thought you said checklists are supposed to *lower* my stress levels. Right now, my blood pressure is shooting through the roof."

Checklists didn't piss you off. You're upset because you didn't have them. If you had the right checklists in place, napkins would be properly folded and placed on each table. That table would be at an exact forty-five-degree angle. And every employee in your restaurant would be concentrating on being as productive as they can for every minute of their shift. Can't waste time socializing when you know you have X number of checklists to complete in X amount of time.

If you haven't seen these results yet, don't worry. That change will come as soon as you get your checklists fixed.

Until then, don't get too attached to whatever you jot down on this first run-through. I've met so many managers who've made the mistake of laminating their checklists like they're set in stone. You could place lines on your dimmer switches showing your staff where you want the lights to be at 5:00 p.m., 8:00 p.m., and 10:00 p.m. and tell them to do it on a checklist—and you'll still walk into your dining room and get upset because the lights aren't at the right levels. Why? Because your checklist doesn't have enough details.

Whatever you've done before, whatever idea you have about checklists inside your mind, think about that, then go one step further. Revise whatever checklists you may have to tell your managers to go online and Google what time sunset is each and every day. Then have them write down the times the lights need to be adjusted instead of using the fixed schedule of 5:00 p.m., 8:00 p.m., and 10:00 p.m. The task could be adjusted to read "One hour before sunset, two hours after sunset, and four hours after sunset" instead. You can't be too specific. Oh, and don't forget to add special-instance rules about topics such as what to do on overcast days.

I know it seems like a lot and, to some, maybe even a little unnecessary, but don't think for one second that I don't follow through on my own advice. Let me tell you, I'm such a strong advocate for checklists that I use them to *manage my own house.*

Anyone who's raised teens, preteens, or even tyrant toddlers can attest to the power struggle known as parenthood. In my case, my career sends me on the road more often than I'd like. I'm literally on the road every month. Sometimes every week of the month. Between presentations and consulting and coaching, I'm not home a lot.

My beautiful wife, Sue, who is the sweetest person in the world, gets frustrated because my kids have cast her into this good cop, bad cop role—but she has to play both. I remember when they were still preteens, and one day, I got a call and she said, "Your children. I've asked them to clean the room and have been nagging them for the last five hours, and I shouldn't have to do that."

I said, "Sue, we need checklists."

She shot the idea down; she didn't think checklists were for children. I tried to explain as best I could that I see the same signs with our kids as I do when I go into these restaurants. Don't be fooled; common sense-itis affects parents too.

Anyway, she didn't bite, so this conversation just kept happening off and on whenever I was on the road. Finally, one day, I was in my home office, working on the computer. Whatever the hell I was working on had me really focused. I don't know if you know what it's like to be business partners with your spouse like I am, but when I looked up, I saw her just standing there in the doorway.

I hate being distracted. I hate having my attention broken when I'm focused on what I'm doing. So without even realizing, I shot her the what-the-hell-do-you-want look. It's one of those things I don't know that I'm doing when I do it—but I did.

Honestly, I didn't know if she was my business partner or my wife at that moment. I mean, I was in my home office, my home *and* my office, so it was hard to create those boundaries.

Anyway, she had her hands on her hips, and when I looked closely, she ... was ... *pissed*. Then husband mode took over, and I asked her what was wrong. She said, "You go deal with him."

I didn't know what she was talking about. She said, "I told your son that you would be upstairs to check him out. I asked him to clean his bathroom." When the kids do something wrong, they are, all of a sudden, specifically my children.

I didn't say a damn word. Before passing judgment, I took my happy little ass up the stairs to see what was going on. I found my innocent-faced preteen and asked him first. He said, "Mom asked me to clean the bathroom." OK, great.

I walked in his bathroom and looked at the sink. Sink looked good. I looked up and—toothpaste spit on two mirrors. I said, "Oh my goodness, buddy, what about this?"

Moved over to the toilet and instantly regretted looking in there. Dust sitting on the top of the toilet, trash on the floor.

"Buddy, how come you didn't do this? Why didn't you clean the mirrors?"

His response? "Mom didn't ask me to do that. She asked me to clean the bathroom."

By his standards, that bathroom was clean. You can't just assume anyone knows what you mean. You need to tell them what *your* standard is.

You have to explain how you want things to look. You need to tell them what you want done and what the end goal should look like.

After recognizing the problem, I decide to take my happy little ass back downstairs and into my home office with a brand-new mission. Enough of the confusion, I knew the solution. We needed checklists.

This was the result.

Initials	Task	Tools
	Mirrors 1. Spray glass cleaner in fine mist 4–6 inches away from the glass 2. Dry off with 2–3 sheets of paper towels, starting at the top of the glass and continuing to the bottom. 3. Throw used paper towels away. **When complete** The glass should be clear: free of smudges, water spots, and any dirt.	• Windex Glass Cleaner • Roll of paper towels

Initials	Task	Tools
	Sink 1. Remove everything from the countertop. 2. Spray bathroom cleaner generously until 50 percent of all surfaces and faucet are covered in foam. 3. With a scrub rag, using pressure, start with the side panels, then the surface including the faucet. Scrub until you get to the bottom of the sink. Scrub until all surfaces are clean and dry. 4. Organize and replace everything removed when you started. **When complete** The sink and faucet should be shiny, smooth, and free of smudges, water spots, and any dirt. The drain cap and ring should be shiny and clean.	• Bathroom surface cleaner • Scrub rags
	Plastic cart 1. Remove everything from the top. 2. Spray glass cleaner or multisurface cleaner in a fine mist 4–6 inches away from the top and all sides. 3. Dry off with clean, dry scrub rags. 4. Organize and replace everything removed when you started. **When complete** The cart should be free of dust and water spots on all sides, ledges, and drawers.	• Windex Glass Cleaner or multisurface cleaner • Scrub rags

Initials	Task	Tools
	Toilet Tank 1. Remove everything from the top of the tank. 2. Spray bathroom cleaner generously until 50 percent of all surfaces, the top, and all three sides are covered in foam. 3. With a scrub rag, using pressure, starting on the top and then the three sides, scrub until you get to the bottom of the tank and all surfaces are clean and dry. **Toilet Lid and seat** 4. Lift the toilet bowl lid and seat, spray bathroom cleaner generously until 50 percent of all surfaces, top and bottom of both, are covered in foam. 5. With a scrub rag, using pressure, starting on the top and then bottom of each, scrub until all surfaces are clean and dry. **Toilet Bowl (Inside)** 6. Spray bathroom cleaner generously until 50 percent of all surfaces inside the bowl are covered in foam and let sit for three minutes. 7. Using a toilet scrub brush with a long handle, start just under the top lip of the inside of the bowl. Scrub with pressure completely around while moving down until the scrub brush is being pushed in and out of the drain. 8. Place handle of brush between seat and bowl to dry.	• Bathroom surface cleaner • Scrub rags • Long-handle toilet bowl scrub brush

Initials	Task	Tools
	Toilet Bowl (Outside) 9. Spray bathroom cleaner generously until 50 percent of all surfaces, on all surfaces of the outer bowl including the floor base, are covered in foam. 10. With a scrub rag, using pressure, starting on the top and then moving down, scrub until you get the outer bowl area clean and dry, including the floor between the wall and the back of the toilet. **Toilet Tank** 11. Organize and replace everything removed when you started. **When complete** The outside of the toilet should be shiny, smooth, and free of smudges, water spots, and any dirt. The inside of the bowl should be clean and should show no water rings or any dirt in the drain.	
	Trash can 1. Empty trash can into a plastic garbage bag, and take the bag outside and place it into the household trash can. **When complete** Trash can should be completely empty of all trash.	• Empty small (15 gallon) white garbage bag
	Cleaners 1. Put all cleaners away under the kitchen sink. 2. Put paper towels back on the kitchen counter by the sink. **When complete** All cleaners and paper towels will be in the kitchen.	

When all tasks are completed, please initial below and have a parent check you out before leaving. Thank you!	
	Kid's initial here stating you have completed all the above tasks
	Parent's initial here stating you have completed all the above tasks

Did you know that it takes eleven steps to clean a toilet in my house? My kids do. Now there's no longer any confusion between all parties involved.

My son doesn't have to read our minds, and as soon as you get your checklists revised, your employees won't have to read yours either. You can't get hysterical at your whole staff because nobody's going to miss something you expected them to do. Managers will feel the pressure lift off their shoulders too. They know what you want done, how you want them to do it, how well, and by when.

I don't care if your checklists end up being ten pages long. I don't care if you have a different process for every day of the week. As a matter of fact, I expect it. Change and tweak your checklists as necessary, but follow-up is key. Once everyone's trained on how to execute the checklists you create, you must hold them to it. I'm guaranteeing near-instantaneous results, but it takes your constant discerning eye to make sure your restaurant is successful.

Just like I'm promising overnight changes, I promise that in about three weeks, once everyone realizes the excitement's died down and you aren't verifying everyone's signature in the binder, managers will stop using them. You're the head coach in this scenario; you have to keep everyone motivated and focused. Communicate your expectations and be painfully clear about everything you expect. When you think you've been detailed enough, find some more details to add. Train your managers on how to push everyone to uphold your standards from open to close every single day. And ultimately, you will hold your management team accountable for all checklists being completed. It's not the line employee's fault they didn't do their side work; that's why you have a manager to ensure the systems are being followed. If the manager doesn't want to get written up, they need to complete the tasks the line employee didn't complete on the checklist. Do other people's side work a few times, and they'll never let anyone go before their work is done.

> You're the head coach in this scenario; you have to keep everyone motivated and focused. Communicate your expectations and be painfully clear about everything you expect.

Cash Controls

Cash handling procedures impact every aspect of your business. If you have poor cash handling procedures in place, none of your other systems will matter. Efficiency is null and void if you aren't depositing every single penny from your restaurant's sales.

Here are some classic errors I see in restaurants:

- **Change in a glass or scattered in the bottom of a drawer.** Most people do this to make night deposits faster because you save time without having to count loose change or to make the night deposit balance equal whatever your point-of-sale (POS) system says.

- **A week's worth of server checkouts in check presenters in an unlocked filing cabinet.** This usually happens when the GM or owner is the only person allowed to make bank runs. It also happens if there isn't enough cash to deposit because of credit card purchases or if the owner/manager is just plain lazy.

- **A bin with a year's worth of used nonvoided paper gift certificates.** Management was right to account for gift certificates the restaurant honors nightly, but without voiding them and by leaving them unsecured, an employee could steal a few every day and reuse them to keep cash sales.

- **Customer checks taped to the office wall.** Lots of restaurants cater or host events, which means you'll take in deposit checks from your customers to cover expenses in case they cancel the reservation. The problem is if you don't deposit them and leave them on display, dishonest employees may be tempted to steal the check or the customer's identity to perform fraud.

- **Credit card numbers recorded in a book.** First off, this is illegal, so it's something we should never see, but sadly enough, we still do. The only place you can legally retain a customer's credit card information is in a secure online record-keeping system permitted by law. Failure to do so could result in astronomical fines.

- **Blank or forged checks for deliveries.** This is another common practice used by owners who need key employees to cover invoices even though they aren't authorized to sign checks. This exposes you to so much liability.

- **Rounding up or down.** Servers hand in cash from their server reports that's rounded to the nearest whole number. Instead of $350.25, they'll turn in $350.00 even when their shift is over.

Don't plant a seed in your employee's mind misleading them to believe that you have money to spare. It's your responsibility to make sure *all* your money makes it into the bank on a daily basis.

Cash handling procedures need to be managed by a trainable system that holds employees accountable for shortages and overages. It needs to become a disciplinary issue that could ultimately cost people their positions in your restaurant. When you put that much weight on cash controls and tie the consequences to their employment, you create a culture that makes counting money accurately more than an expectation—it's a rule.

I've had quite a successful career in the restaurant industry, and I made a decent name for myself in comedy way back locally as well. I've been tossing around the idea of launching a new business venture—I think I might take up rapping. You're never too old to chase a dream, right?

I've been brainstorming this for a while, and I think I finally came up with the perfect rap name: 63 Cent.

How's that sound?

C'mon, you know I'd be blazing the stage. I can hear the DJ now. "Everybody put your hands in the air and give it up for our next performer—*63 Cent!*" The crowd would go crazy! I already know it.

OK, I'm kidding. But if I did choose to drop a few bars, 63 Cent would be the perfect name because I want it *all.*

I want to know where every penny is. That's *cash control*—a culture where the details matter. I want to make sure plates are clean and checklists and cash controls are in place that make it clear that if a server report says you owe me $323.63, I want my $0.63. Don't try to casually hand me $323.00. There's no rounding up or rounding down in the restaurant world.

You must create a culture where the details matter because it sets a standard for your staff. Give me my $0.63 to show you understand that I'm paying attention to everything, down to the last penny. Give me my damn $0.63 so that good people aren't tempted to turn into thieves.

If you can't get your people to pay attention to these types of details, there's no way in hell you're going to convince them to wake up in the morning and get excited about going to work to count inventory. It's up to you to do the groundwork so your restaurant can start benefiting from some powerful systems that will help you make more money than you ever have before.

CHAPTER TAKEAWAYS

- With systems in place, your managers will never get in trouble again.

- Detailed checklists are essential to the success of your business.

- "Every Penny Matters"—rapper 63 Cent's next hit record.

CHAPTER 6

A SINGLE SYSTEM CAN SAVE YOU 5–10 PERCENT

You're only as good as your weakest department. For your restaurant to be successful, your entire operation needs to move like a well-oiled machine. With every aspect of your business depending on the next, it's important for restaurant owners to perfect the ideal combination of three main gears:

1. numbers,

2. people, and

3. menu.

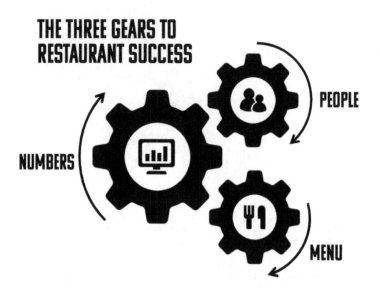

THE THREE GEARS TO RESTAURANT SUCCESS

NUMBERS

PEOPLE

MENU

I know you've spent some time thinking about how the big chain restaurants do it without having owners walking the floor all day long. They do it by using these three gears to perform a checkup on their business. Evaluating each section on its own and as part of the restaurant's entire operation helps owners fine-tune whatever areas appear as the restaurant's weakest link.

You can have the best products and service in the world, but without keeping the numbers in line, your business will eventually close its doors.

You can have an incredible menu and the numbers drilled down to a science, but if your service sucks, you'll run your business into the ground.

Great service from great people with great numbers (all your controls are in place) with a crappy menu means you're going out of business.

You're only as strong as your weakest link.

The systems you create help you impose your will without being inside the restaurant twenty-four hours a day. I don't care if you have one restaurant or two or three—you should be working *on* your business rather than in it.

Let's take the personalities out of the equation. Let's remove common sense-itis too. Let's leave nothing to chance or an outdated routine and revolutionize the way you run your business.

It all boils down to consistency. And having a budget.

It's Time to Erase Your Fear of Budgets

The word *budget* should not send chills running down your spine. If you're scared of your restaurant's budget, I'm 100 percent sure you're losing money and you don't even know it.

Budgets aren't fun, but they're necessary. How will you know what success looks like if you don't set your standards for it? (For your information, industry standards don't apply. This is strictly about success according to your own definition!)

I've been all around the world to speak about how systems will change the face of the independent restaurant industry for good. In 99 percent of my speeches, you'll hear me talk about the two most important systems any restaurant can have: budgets and recipe cards.

Guess what two systems most restaurants never have? Budgets and recipe cards.

> Spare me the excuses. Cry me a river. Budgets are hard. Life will become a whole lot harder if you don't start getting your finances in order.

Spare me the excuses. Cry me a river. Budgets are hard. Life will become a whole lot harder if you don't start getting your finances in order.

I mean it. This is serious business, and I don't think most independent owners even realize how much they're screwing themselves when they treat their budget like an option on their to-do list. Whenever I hear, "David, budgets are so hard!" I say, "Tough shit. Buck up, man. You're in the toughest business I know." The truth isn't always wrapped in a pretty package, but those owners understand what I mean by the time they're finished with my coaching program.

Budgets and recipe cards are so critical to your success because these two systems move you away from reactive management and place you in a proactive position, just as I learned while teaching at the Scottsdale Culinary Institute. This is how you set your standards. This is how you focus on accountability. To hell with industry averages, your budget should be custom made specifically for your business.

Back in the day, I used to preach that every restaurant needs a budget for the next three to five years. Now I know that the next twelve months should be the main focus for your business.

Five years is entirely too long; your budget needs to be flexible. It should be based on your restaurant's specific operation and the seasonality of your sales.

The budget creates the basis for your COGS and labor targets. Heck, all your financial targets, if you really think about it. Without these, you wouldn't even be able to steer your business throughout the year. We all know how dreaded they are; I mean, most restaurant owners I meet try to turn themselves invisible whenever I mention the *B* word. They hear *budget* and their heads start to spin, and they start sweating and stuttering and becoming all anxious. Many go into overdrive, and rather than really understanding the reason why budgets are so important, they throw their hands in the air and try to work out some sort of budget with their gut. At the end of all that, they'll have something to look at, but a budget filled with guesses isn't enough; you need real numbers.

Following a proper budget will place you on a profitable path. Of course there'll be some missteps along the way, but whenever you notice a discrepancy in your results versus the budget, just crunch the numbers again, then fix the system that created the error. At no point is it ever OK to let your budget go unchecked. As a matter of fact, I think we need to talk about the steps to starting an accurate budget. Let's get to that next.

Budget Process

STEP ONE: FORECAST YOUR SALES

I've created a tool, essentially an intuitive spreadsheet, called the "Restaurant Sales Forecast Generator." It's an easy-to-use tool to help you forecast your sales by day of the week for any month or specific period you identify in the system. All you have to do is plug in your numbers using the SWAG forecast (that is, a scientific wild-ass guess). Using the Restaurant Sales Forecast Generator is really easy for existing restaurant owners. For you, the forecast science will come from your actual sales history to start. Then the guessing part comes in as you try to figure out whether your sales are trending up or down and, ultimately, what your best guess is on what's going to happen with your sales going forward.

You have to forecast because without it, you won't know how much food you can buy or how many people you can schedule to work.

Bring too many people on the same shift, and tick, tick, tick, that labor clock starts adding up quicker than you know. If you open your doors understaffed, you'll probably have long ticket times and bad service, and you'll probably still lose money by the minute due to lost opportunities.

Buy too much food and it'll get stolen, spoil, and go to waste, and you'll still lose money. If you don't buy enough, you'll have to eighty-six items off the menu, which will piss off your guests and cause lost opportunities to make money.

Everything begins with a solid sales forecast. There's no way around it.

STEP TWO: UNDERSTANDING PRIME COST

For decades, restaurants have been run with one key number in mind. This magic number ensures that the owners make money. It's called "prime cost." To old-timers like me, it used to be called "controllable expenses," those expenses that are in the control of management on a daily basis because of how they hire, fire, and schedule their team members to how they purchase and use products. For all intents and purposes, it's your manager's report card.

To get an accurate prime cost, you must calculate it using an accrual accounting system. Because you have inventory on your shelves, the government requires you to file your tax returns using accrual accounting anyway.

Accrual accounting is comprised of the concept "earn, owe, use."

Earn. All sales, collected or not, are recorded the day they happen. Almost all restaurants calculate this number daily. With accrual accounting, whether or not cash or a check has been received, the sale is recorded on the day it occurred, not the day it was deposited.

Owe. Any time a product crosses your restaurant's back door, paid for or not, it is recorded as an expense for that day. Here's where restaurants mess up their prime cost calculations. Where most restaurants fall off the tracks on this is with the expense showing up only after the bill has been paid, which can be many days or even months later, making the COGS look out of whack.

When it comes to your labor costs, it's the salaries and wages for the actual days that you're using for your prime cost calculation date range.

Use. As it sounds, this is what you used in product. For instance, if you sell a burger, you've used an eight-ounce hamburger patty, two slices of tomato, two ounces of shredded lettuce, a bun, and so on. It doesn't matter how many cases of hamburger patties you purchased, COGS *only* includes the food product that actually left your shelves to bring in sales. If you purchased more than you actually used, food purchases will be moved from the expense onto your balance sheet as an asset in inventory and vice versa: if you use more than you purchased, you will move inventory dollars down to expenses to show that your food cost is actually higher.

I know you don't want to hear it, but this means you need to be doing inventory *at least* once a month, and I'll have you taking inventory weekly.

Again, regarding labor, if you're on a calendar year accounting cycle, twelve months versus, say, a thirteen-period accounting cycle, and you're paying your team members every other week, there will be times where a single pay period has only a portion of it in one accounting period and the rest in the next period. While it won't be perfectly accurate, you need to show the labor expense in the period it happened and make that adjustment. An easy calendar accounting workaround to this is paying paychecks on a semimonthly basis. This way both payrolls fit perfectly in the month they happened.

I don't care what else you take from this book, but I need your undivided attention while we're covering prime cost.

What is prime cost?

prime cost = total cost of goods sold (COGS) + total labor cost

That's your magic number.

If you want any chance at making money in the restaurant business, you need to know your prime cost. Most owners don't know it and have no idea where to begin to calculate it. That's why I'm here to help you. I want to make sure you have all the tools you need to be successful.

Let's start with the first part of the equation: *COGS*.

That's the food cost, pour cost (or in layman's terms, liquor cost), and merchandise cost. This is the cost of the products you sell. Bottled beer, draft beer, wine, liquor, all the food on your menu, and the merchandise you sell.

Most people don't know their food cost or pour cost because they try to take shortcuts when calculating their COGS. They take their purchases and divide them by their sales, but that number is inaccurate.

When calculating your COGS, you need to account for *everything* that leaves your shelves. What did you actually use? You can't just focus on what you purchased.

One month, you could buy a lot of product, but since it wasn't used, you'll find yourself low on cash and your shelves full. Confused, you could look at your food cost to identify the problem, but your food cost isn't what's high. On the flip side of that coin, you could only buy a little product, and when you measure it against your purchases, you think your food costs are low. Truth of the matter is you depleted $2,000 more than you purchased from your inventory, and your food cost is actually high. The real challenge in this case is most restaurant owners won't even look to see there is a problem because their bank account will more than likely be healthy.

That's why taking accurate inventory is so important. I know it's difficult. It can take some people hours to get their inventory done. To get around that, I teach owners how to set up a shelf-to-sheet inventory system where they can take inventory in under one hour to calculate COGS. To calculate your actual COGS, the formula is

cost of goods sold (use) = beginning inventory + purchases – ending inventory.

Look, if you don't take inventories for value, and I'm going to make that assumption, please know you're not dead in the water. You can calculate your COGS by using a year, the past twelve months of purchases, divided into the last twelve months of sales by category. This is your COGS. The change in inventory over the course of twelve months is so small, it won't skew the numbers by much.

cost of goods sold% = use ÷ sales

Now let's move on to the second half of the equation: *labor cost.*

Labor cost is all expenses accrued when people clock in and out at their registers plus taxes, benefits, and insurance. It includes whatever you're paying your salaried managers. Regarding owners' salaries, it gets a bit tricky.

Do you, the owner, belong in prime cost too?

As the owner/operator, you may or may not belong in prime cost. In the case that you've been busting your butt as a manager on the floor, your salary or an adjusted amount of your salary is a part of your prime cost. Why? Because when I get you to the point where you're working *on* your business instead of in it, you'll be paying someone else that salary.

For example, if I pay myself $75,000, but the market says I should be paying a manager $50,000, that $50,000 salary is a part of my prime cost. The other $25,000 is just sucking up profits and is a part of operating expenses, not labor, even though it may be paid in payroll.

If I only work two days a week, two-fifths of my salary, or an adjusted two-fifths, belongs in prime cost. Be mindful, though, because other salaries like those for an on-staff bookkeeper or marketing person are not a part of prime cost. Prime cost is *only* made up of whomever it takes to run the shifts.

Add your total labor cost to your total COGS: that will tell you what your prime cost is.

From there, the next step is to divide your total, or prime cost, into your *gross sales* (not net sales). That's sales before discounts, not including sales tax. It's important to understand the difference between gross and net sales.

Gross sales. This is the ring at the register before discounts are taken out, without adding in sales tax. (Sales tax isn't a sale. It's just the privilege the government gives us of holding their money for them—and then they penalize us like the mob if we don't pay them back.)

For example, if you ring up a $10 burger and comp $5, the gross sale is $10, not including sales tax.

Net sales. This is what you ring at the register minus discounts and without adding in sales tax.

For example, that same $10 burger, with a $5 comp, will land me $5 in net sales.

You must track and use gross sales to get accurate measurements of your manager's performance. Be careful: what most POS systems label as gross sales is actually net sales—sales less discounts. Make sure you're using the right numbers.

But you're not done yet.

For most of my restaurant career, I was taught—and taught others—that key prime cost targets were 65 percent for full-service restaurants and 60 percent for quick service. With this number in mind, I never had a problem helping restaurant owners consistently hit the 60 percent target. Now I know that number's no good.

Thanks to the Great Recession and all the shit the food service industry took as a result, food prices rise all the time and minimum wage is shooting through the roof. This means your margins are shrinking by the day. I'm no economist, and I'm not a certified public account, but I am a restaurant expert who knows our industry inside and out. What I can tell you is if your restaurant is doing at least $850,000 a year, your new prime cost target is 55 percent, and it's 60 percent if your sales are lower than $850,000 a year.

You probably think I've lost my damn mind, but trust me, it's 55 percent. I'm coaching owners hitting that target every single day and many hitting targets way under that. They aren't doing anything that you yourself can't start doing and seeing the same results with, if not better.

Let's look at some of the processes they're following and how it's benefiting their bottom line.

MENU

- **Budgeted purchasing.** I teach a purchase allotment system I call the "Restaurant Checkbook Guardian" that in combination with two clipboard systems (the key item tracker and waste tracker) has reduced owners' food costs by 2–3 percent and reduced the inventory of every restaurant owner (and I mean every single one) I've talked to. And it basically happened overnight. Why? Because their chef can only spend what has been budgeted. They can no longer just order because they think they need it. This makes your cooks take better care of what's on the shelves because there isn't an abundance of supplies available, and it gives you back control of your bank account. From that point on, they'll have to ask you for permission if they need to spend more than what was budgeted.

- **Prime vendor agreement.** If you promise to purchase 90 percent of your products from one broadline distributor, you'll almost always save 3–7 percent. I can help you with that.

- **Menu analysis.** Restaurants see a minimum of 3–7 percent reduction in food costs the first time I go through the menu engineering process because they learn how this process can easily assist with strategically raising their prices, making smarter purchases, dropping items from the menu, and so on—all profit-friendly decisions.

LABOR

- **Budgeted labor.** My labor allotment system, called the "Restaurant Payroll Guardian," offers owners a minimum reduction in labor cost by at least 1–2 percent. Some see savings as high as 10-plus percent. This system not only tells each manager how much money they have for the upcoming work week but also how many hours they have to schedule by position.

They quickly see when they have overscheduled based on sales forecasts and can adjust the schedule before it's posted.

- **Tracking.** Daily tracking allows management to make small changes throughout the week to stick to the budget. You will no longer get to Friday and start screaming, "*Cut, cut, cut!*" because you just noticed you're dramatically over budget and have to cut team members when you need them most on your busiest shifts of the week.

- **Training.** With my training systems, owners reduce labor costs thanks to lower turnover rates and increased sales, which come from happy guests.

Listen, creating your budget and identifying what financial changes you need to make isn't going to change who you are. Your core values will keep everything in check. In other words, if you identify you need to lower your food cost, you're not going to buy crappy product when your core values include quality.

Now, 55 percent prime cost doesn't sound like a fairy tale, does it?

Prime cost is and always will be one of the most critical elements for your business, but you must believe in its possibility. Because if you think it's not possible, you're right. It's called a self-fulfilling prophecy.

Another owner I coached, Steve Brown, counted out his own bar drawers every morning for twenty-four straight years. He didn't know where his prime cost was—let alone where it should be. He didn't have recipe cards. He didn't have many systems to control his margins in place. The systems he learned from me and then began using took him far from the way he'd grown accustomed to doing business when he opened in the eighties. Now Steve's operating at a 42 percent prime cost and his fingers haven't touched the bar drawer since. He's got a whole management team, trained managers, and tailored systems. He's making more money than he ever has, and I couldn't be prouder of him.

That's what I do. I know how powerful my systems are. You have to believe change is possible; otherwise, it's not.

And you must be willing to do the work.

STEP THREE: CALCULATING FIXED AND VARIABLE EXPENSES

Now it's time to figure out the rest of your budget or should I say, your *operating expenses*. Some expenses are fixed, meaning they stay the same every month, such as salaried managers. Others are variable expenses, expenses that go up and down with sales, like hourly team members.

For example, if 10 percent of your sales is budgeted for line cook labor, for every $1.00 that comes into your restaurant, $0.10 is being spent on cooks. If you sell $100,000 in a month, that's $10,000 you have to spend on cooks. If you boost your sales to $200,000 or $300,000, you have a lot more money to spend on cooks. If you miss your target, you don't have as much to spend on them. It's important to understand your limits.

There are some expenses that can be either/or, like the rent for your location. Variable leases could include terms like 7 percent of gross sales. If you've partnered with your landlord, then that's a variable expense. If you've got a lease for $10,000 per month no matter what your sales, then your lease is fixed.

Go down the list, and calculate all your average fixed expenses using the equation:

average fixed expenses = total annual fixed expenses ÷ 12.

That'll give you the number for your monthly average fixed expense. Add it to your budget.

Do the same for your variable expenses—one by one.

For example,

average variable paper goods expense = total annual paper goods costs ÷ total gross sales.

The dividend will give you the estimated percentage of your paper goods costs, say, 2.5 percent. You'd just plug that number into the template until you've covered all your variable expenses too.

• • • • • • • • • • •

SECTION QUICK CHECK

- Twelve months of sales (Check your POS system, QuickBooks, or whatever spreadsheet you use.)

- Twelve months COGS (COGS = (cost of purchases − ending used) ÷ sales)

- Twelve months of labor costs (Check your payroll reports, and make sure you only add prime cost labor.)

• • • • • • • • • • •

All your fixed and variable expenses over the last twelve months divided by twelve or your sales will show you where you stand today. Use those numbers to forecast, or budget, your restaurant's activity for the next twelve months.

Just remember, if you do what you've always done, you'll get what you've always gotten.

Another thing to note, don't get hung up on technicalities like fiscal years. If we're talking about your business today, we'd start looking at your sales records from this month, counting twelve months back because we're going to create a budget for the next twelve months. Then it's time to face the music.

STEP FOUR: BE PROACTIVE!

One of the key benefits of taking the steps to create your budget is embracing a proactive position rather than a reactive one.

What numbers are you using to create your budget? For most people, they're looking at their profit and loss (P&L) statement for the past twelve months.

Now, let's think about this. What does the P&L represent?

The past! And last time I checked, you can't change the past. So why do people spend so much time focused on it? Don't get me wrong, your P&L, when used correctly, is your report card on how you are operating your business. But think of it this way: running a business by a P&L is like driving a car with the front windshield completely blacked out and only using the rearview mirror as your guide. Try that if you'd like. You'll earn a 100 percent chance of crashing into something.

The P&L gives you a good glimpse of your past, but it's the future that's going to put money in your pocket.

Now, with a budget, you can peel away the black window tint on your windshield and start driving while facing forward. The only thing the rearview mirror is good for is to remind you of where you've been. The P&L gives you a good glimpse of your past, but it's the future that's going to put money in your pocket.

Running your restaurant only using your P&L is like only using your rearview mirror. That's why budgeting is so important. Rather than leave your future profits up to chance, let me show you how to take that budget and update it so it's more relevant.

Once you have whatever budget template you use available, that's when the real fun begins.

I want you to look at your budget template and ask yourself, If I operate my restaurant the exact same way as I have for the last twelve months these next twelve months, am I going to make or lose money, and how much?

I don't care what your answer is; I want you to look at your budget like it's covered in snot. Yuck! Ew! It's not good enough.

Now it's time to be proactive.

If you've never worked with me before, I know for a fact that if you implement the key item tracker and waste tracker, which are two simple clipboard systems, plus a purchase allotment system (the Restaurant Checkbook Guardian), you'll be able to drop your food cost two to three percentage points overnight. That's even before we get into recipe cards, inventory, and all the other controls I show people how to implement and train others on.

What that means is you could regain two to three points just by paying attention.

When you bring me your budget template, I'll be able to see where we need to begin to reorganize your operation to be more profitable and efficient. I'd evaluate your numbers and say, "We're going to train these systems in month 1, and on month 2, we're going to hold your managers accountable to these systems and drop food cost by three points."

Then I could keep the diagnosis going. "OK, now you need to start using recipe costing cards. That's going to take forty-to-sixty man hours. How long will it take you to get that done? Two months? OK, by month 3, I'll do an analysis on your menu and your product mix. We'll be able to figure out what your ideal food cost should be."

When that's all said and done, I would reengineer the restaurant's menu. Then by the time we hit month 4, I'd have them put a brand-new menu on the table: one that's been specially designed based on where that restaurant's prime cost is and where it needs to be. We're talking about maximizing your profitability by reducing your food cost another five points just from putting out a new menu.

Let's say your food cost last year was 34 percent, and that was your budget's starting point. Following the systems we just talked about, in month 2, your food cost would be 31 percent, and by month 4 it would decrease to about 26 percent. It seems so much more complicated than it really is. The hardest part is knowing what to look for and how to fix it. In all my years, I have to say, nothing produces the same results as a well-constructed system. Such a system can transform budgets from being some scary bogey monster hiding in your office into a workable plan that helps your restaurant make more money.

Wouldn't you like to be able to put a little something extra away in your savings?

The plans you make using your budget will help you achieve that goal—as long as we keep our attention fixed on working with real numbers and with a hint of intuition. Do that, and you'll have a plan that identifies systems with the potential to boost your profits. Taking things a step further, if you put your budget beside your P&L at the end of each period, you can tell exactly where you've been missing your target or staying on track.

If you fell short, was it because your managers aren't using the damn systems you put in place? If so, it's time to retrain them and hold them accountable for their decisions.

If everybody's been following the systems, what new systems do you need to put in place?

And here's the big benefit: if you were supposed to make $7,000 in month 2 but you only made $4,000, what small adjustments can you make over the next ten months to make up for that $3,000 loss without sacrificing the quality you deliver to your guests?

Instead of freezing when you fall short, the only thing that you can do is adjust your plan and get back on track. And remember, you don't need to give up on guest satisfaction, cut the quality of your products, or go against somebody's core values. Just use the numbers to become a proactive manager.

CHAPTER TAKEAWAYS

- Create a proactive budget based on *your* numbers, not industry averages.

- Prime cost is one of the most important equations you'll work with. Make sure you're using the right numbers to measure it.

- If you miss your budgeted target, make small adjustments to recover that loss throughout the rest of the year.

CHAPTER 7

THREE SIMPLE SYSTEMS TO SHAVE FOOD COST AND SAVE MONEY

Now let's talk about managing your number one asset—your cash.

Think about all the inventory sitting on your shelves. What is all that?

I remember back when I worked for one of the worst, Napoleon, little SOB managers I've ever worked under in my life. I hated everything about him, so you can imagine how I felt when, one day, he walks my ass into a walk-in cooler and says, "David, what do you see?"

In my mind, I'm like, "Duh, food … " Right?

Wrong.

That wasn't the answer. It was money.

This example proves you can learn something from anyone if you keep an open mind.

Remember that when you're walking around your restaurant, worrying about the $300 cash deposit at the end of the night, you've got thousands upon thousands of dollars sitting around your restaurant in unlocked areas, like a welcome invitation. Some of you may as well put a bow on your shelves because you have employees treating your stockroom like it's Christmas.

Well, last time I checked, I can't go to the power company with a case of steaks and go, "Thud! We're even."

Too much inventory means less money in the bank to pay for the things you need. You have to create a company culture around respecting the value of your inventory.

When you're yelling at the chef about an item they eighty-sixed, don't teach them that buying more is the right solution to that problem. You need to train them about waste and spoilage instead. Don't just toss fries on a plate; verify portioning is being done like you trained.

Too much product raises your risk of waste and spoilage. When your line cooks see that there's plenty of food on the shelves, they don't treat your product as special. That's not half a case of tomatoes you're throwing away week after week because you're ordering too much, it's money down the drain. It keeps happening because nobody's paying attention.

You don't need a week's worth of food on the shelves—only three to four days, max. That's enough to get you from one delivery to the next and still have plenty on the shelves to handle the busload of people who actually pull up to your restaurant and walk in unexpectedly. When your inventory's overstocked, it's no wonder you can't pay yourself or make payroll.

That's your money getting chucked into the trash. That's your money with an expiration date printed on it. Money wouldn't expire if it was in the bank like it was supposed to be.

Consider this chapter a direct attack on your food cost or any of your COGS categories. It's time for you to start earning the money you deserve, even if that means going back to the drawing board and retraining some old processes.

In our industry, the most common way to fix a problem is to throw money at it and hope it'll go away. Every day, we get slapped in the face by profit-eating mistakes like food missing off the shelves because of overportioning, waste, and theft. What do most people think the solution is? Need more, buy more; the easiest way to find your accounts in the red is to write the check without finding out why you're spending so much.

> Need more, buy more; the easiest way to find your accounts in the red is to write the check without finding out why you're spending so much.

Instead of actually looking for the problem, people just spend money like it grows on trees. You hand over total control of your checkbook and, in turn, sacrifice all opportunity to make a decent profit. Let's start working on adding a few money-saving systems to your operation.

Three Money-Saving Systems

You'd be amazed by the way simple clipboard systems and a little data can lower your food cost by three points overnight. That's another guarantee from me to you.

Without any heavy lifting or major systems in place, all you need is three simple systems:

- the key item tracker,

- the waste tracker, and

- the purchase allotment system (Restaurant Checkbook Guardian).

THE KEY ITEM TRACKER

This is a straightforward clipboard system that requires you to count your inventory at the beginning and end of the shift or day, depending on how much control you want to have. It's the best way to catch a thief before they ramp up their momentum. You'll be counting/tracking five to fifteen items on a shift-by-shift or daily basis. You'll account for every single item that you want to control.

Here's how it works. You start with a beginning count of, let's say, twelve 8 oz. filets. Let's say you prep an additional six because it's a busy night. That means you have a potential eighteen filets ready to be sold. At the end of the shift, or day, you will go to your POS system and find out how many filets you sold. Let's say it's ten. Eighteen filets minus ten sold says you should have eight filets still in your drawer. Now you take your happy little ass over to the drawer and count what is actually there. If you count six, six minus eight says there are two missing.

If something's missing, check the waste tracker. If you can't find it there, then one of two things happened—someone stole it or, worse, your managers aren't using the systems you laid out for them to control your numbers.

By using this system, you virtually eliminate the theft of any of the items you track on a shift or daily basis because your cooks understand that they could easily be caught. The waste tracker helps you fill in the blanks when you're wondering where all your food, I mean *money*, is going.

THE WASTE TRACKER

Here's another simple clipboard system that allows employees to keep track of every time they waste a product. Remember, if something got burnt on the stove, if it fell on the floor, if the tomatoes went bad—anything that's been wasted gets recorded.

The waste tracker makes sure everyone keeps track of their mistakes. If you have a server double order by mistake and you mark it down, you can quickly start to see the need for retraining—or termination if they are doing it to be able to eat for free because your management team is allowing people to eat the mistakes. If a cook is burning steaks again, decide to retrain or terminate. This process is a lot better than coming to your chef fifteen days into the next period after getting your P&L, wondering why your food cost is so high. The waste sheet gives you a chance to say, "Today, we made a mistake. Let's fix it so we don't do it again tomorrow." This process helps you take a proactive approach to food cost control.

Behind the bar, it's sometimes known as a spill sheet; it's the same thing. Bartenders hate it. Everyone hates it. It reminds me of a book titled *Games People Play* originally published in 1964 by psychiatrist Eric Berne. No, I never read it, but my dad did, and he taught me something I'll always remember from this book. People in the workplace like to play a game called NIGYYSOB. What's that mean?

"Now I've got you, you son of a bitch."

Employees avoid the waste tracker because they're scared to lose their jobs, and they don't want to show you that they screwed up. You must calm those fears by changing your company culture.

Waste trackers aren't for punishment; they identify opportunities to train your people, to purchase smarter and more. You can reposition people or terminate them if they just don't change. You can be proactive about the way you run your restaurant.

I don't care if it's a Friday night in the middle of your busy season. Don't tell me why it can't be done; tell me *how* it can be done. When you are ten tickets deep, you might just throw the mistakes into a clear Lexan at the end of the line, and at the end of the shift, make it like an archeological dig and write them down after the rush.

THE PURCHASE ALLOTMENT SYSTEM (RESTAURANT CHECKBOOK GUARDIAN)

Here's where we really bite into the meat of your systems.

Let me tell you, this system is one of the most powerful things I teach. Even without getting into the power of recipe cards, you can use your sales forecast and your target COGS and keep track of your daily sales, daily invoices—stuff you're supposed to do every day anyway—to predict how much you have to spend on your next order.

> Stop fixing your problems by writing checks; there's an underlying issue that needs to be addressed.

The purchase allotment system allows managers to take over and gives the owner permission to hand over the responsibility without giving up your checkbook.

Stop fixing your problems by writing checks; there's an underlying issue that needs to be addressed.

The next time your manager comes up to you and says, "Our next order is going to be really high. I know it's a lot, but we need it, we've got a busy weekend coming up," you shouldn't respond by handing over a blank check. You need to pay attention to the little details.

Ask questions! Why do you need more food? Check the waste tracker. Track your daily sales. Look at the key item tracker, and start making changes.

The purchase allotment system hands over ordering control with a specific budget to follow. You can give them a little wiggle room, but if you say, "You may order up to $500.00 more," by the time they hit $500.01, they can't place the order without your approval.

Your managers need to be prepared to find the problem, fix it, and tell you what they did. Even still, you may not be able to approve the order because, at the end of the day, cash pays the bills, profits don't.

CREATING A PURCHASE ALLOTMENT SYSTEM

Bear in mind, the purchase allotment system needs be used in conjunction with standardized purchasing systems to gain the best results. It allows management to order what's needed to keep operations smooth while staying within the budget you've laid out for them. Should problems arise—and they probably will—they can look at the purchase allotment system to identify there's a problem and correct them today.

There are four rules that are critical to its success:

Rule 1. COGS targets must be (properly) budgeted.

Rule 2. Inventory levels must be worked up and down to hit your targets.

Rule 3. Sales forecasts must be created for each day of the month.

Rule 4. Sales must be tracked by major category on a daily basis.

Do this, and at the start of each month, you will fill in your purchase allotment system as follows:

1. Enter the daily projection for the forecasted sales.

YEAR	2019	MONTH	NOV ▾	FOOD					
Mix Total	0.00%	Remove Blanks		MIX	0.00%	TARGET	0.00%		
Forecasted Sales	Actual Sales Total	DATE	DAY	Forecasted Food Sales	Actual Food Sales	Food Allotment	Actually Spent	Raw Food Cost %	Estimated Order
	0.00	2019-11-01	Fri	0.00		0.00		0.00%	0.00
	0.00	2019-11-02	Sat	0.00		0.00		0.00%	0.00
	0.00	2019-11-03	Sun	0.00		0.00		0.00%	0.00
	0.00	2019-11-04	Mon	0.00		0.00		0.00%	0.00
	0.00	2019-11-05	Tue	0.00		0.00		0.00%	0.00
	0.00	2019-11-06	Wed	0.00		0.00		0.00%	0.00
	0.00	2019-11-07	Thu	0.00		0.00		0.00%	0.00
	0.00	2019-11-08	Fri	0.00		0.00		0.00%	0.00
	0.00	2019-11-09	Sat	0.00		0.00		0.00%	0.00
	0.00	2019-11-10	Sun	0.00		0.00		0.00%	0.00

2. Enter the sales mix percentage for each major sales category individually to equal 100 percent.

YEAR	2019	MONTH	NOV ▾	FOOD					
Mix Total	100.00%	Remove Blanks		MIX	80.00%	TARGET	0.00%		
Forecasted Sales	Actual Sales Total	DATE	DAY	Forecasted Food Sales	Actual Food Sales	Food Allotment	Actually Spent	Raw Food Cost %	Estimated Order
4,313.70	0.00	2019-11-01	Fri	3,450.96		0.00		0.00%	0.00
4,268.33	0.00	2019-11-02	Sat	3,414.66		0.00		0.00%	0.00
2,347.95	0.00	2019-11-03	Sun	1,878.36		0.00		0.00%	0.00
2,227.97	0.00	2019-11-04	Mon	1,782.38		0.00		0.00%	0.00
2,310.80	0.00	2019-11-05	Tue	1,848.64		0.00		0.00%	0.00
2,967.10	0.00	2019-11-06	Wed	2,373.68		0.00		0.00%	0.00
4,418.65	0.00	2019-11-07	Thu	3,534.92		0.00		0.00%	0.00
4,313.70	0.00	2019-11-08	Fri	3,450.96		0.00		0.00%	0.00
4,268.33	0.00	2019-11-09	Sat	3,414.66		0.00		0.00%	0.00
2,347.95	0.00	2019-11-10	Sun	1,878.36		0.00		0.00%	0.00

3. Enter the target COGS percent for each major sales category individually.

YEAR	2019	MONTH	NOV ▾	FOOD					
Mix Total	100.00%	Remove Blanks		MIX	80.00%	TARGET	28.00%		
Forecasted Sales	Actual Sales Total	DATE	DAY	Forecasted Food Sales	Actual Food Sales	Food Allotment	Actually Spent	Raw Food Cost %	Estimated Order
4,313.70	0.00	2019-11-01	Fri	3,450.96		966.27		0.00%	966.27
4,268.33	0.00	2019-11-02	Sat	3,414.66		956.11		0.00%	1,922.37
2,347.95	0.00	2019-11-03	Sun	1,878.36		525.94		0.00%	2,448.32
2,227.97	0.00	2019-11-04	Mon	1,782.38		499.07		0.00%	2,947.38
2,310.80	0.00	2019-11-05	Tue	1,848.64		517.62		0.00%	3,465.00
2,967.10	0.00	2019-11-06	Wed	2,373.68		664.63		0.00%	4,129.63
4,418.65	0.00	2019-11-07	Thu	3,534.92		989.78		0.00%	5,119.41
4,313.70	0.00	2019-11-08	Fri	3,450.96		966.27		0.00%	6,085.68
4,268.33	0.00	2019-11-09	Sat	3,414.66		956.11		0.00%	7,041.78
2,347.95	0.00	2019-11-10	Sun	1,878.36		525.94		0.00%	7,567.72

4. Calculate category allotment individually by multiplying the projected forecasted category sales by the target COGS percent.

**target COGS percent × forecasted category
sales = category allotment**

Forecasted Sales	Actual Sales Total	DATE	DAY	Forecasted Food Sales	Actual Food Sales	Food Allotment	Actually Spent	Raw Food Cost %	Estimated Order
4,313.70	0.00	2019-11-01	Fri	3,450.96		966.27		0.00%	966.27
4,268.33	0.00	2019-11-02	Sat	3,414.66		956.11		0.00%	1,922.37
2,347.95	0.00	2019-11-03	Sun	1,878.36		525.94		0.00%	2,448.32
2,227.97	0.00	2019-11-04	Mon	1,782.38		499.07		0.00%	2,947.38
2,310.80	0.00	2019-11-05	Tue	1,848.64		517.62		0.00%	3,465.00
2,967.10	0.00	2019-11-06	Wed	2,373.68		664.63		0.00%	4,129.63
4,418.65	0.00	2019-11-07	Thu	3,534.92		989.78		0.00%	5,119.41
4,313.70	0.00	2019-11-08	Fri	3,450.96		966.27		0.00%	6,085.68
4,268.33	0.00	2019-11-09	Sat	3,414.66		956.11		0.00%	7,041.78
2,347.95	0.00	2019-11-10	Sun	1,878.36		525.94		0.00%	7,567.72

(YEAR 2019 MONTH NOV — Mix Total 100.00% — MIX 80.00% — TARGET FOOD 28.00%)

This establishes a theoretical COGS for each category. If you hit the daily category sales goals in each list, theoretically, you would have used the dollar value in product listed in the category allotment column.

5. At the end of each day, enter the actual category sales and calculate the appropriate category allotment for each row. (In a perfect world, this is the dollar value of the product that you actually used to generate those sales.)

**target COGS percent × actual category
sales = category allotment**

Forecasted Sales	Actual Sales Total	DATE	DAY	Forecasted Food Sales	Actual Food Sales	Food Allotment	Actually Spent	Raw Food Cost %	Estimated Order
4,313.70	2,897.33	2019-11-01	Fri	3,450.96	2,897.33	811.25		0.00%	811.25
4,268.33	3,544.77	2019-11-02	Sat	3,414.66	3,544.77	992.54		0.00%	803.79
2,347.95	3,025.88	2019-11-03	Sun	1,878.36	3,025.88	847.25		0.00%	2,651.03
2,227.97	4,688.01	2019-11-04	Mon					0.00%	3,963.68
2,310.80	2,045.33	2019-11-05	Tue	1,848.64	2,045.33	572.69		0.00%	4,536.37
2,967.10	0.00	2019-11-06	Wed	2,373.68		664.63		0.00%	5,201.00
4,418.65	0.00	2019-11-07	Thu	3,534.92		989.78		0.00%	6,190.78
4,313.70	0.00	2019-11-08	Fri	3,450.96		966.27		0.00%	7,157.05
4,268.33	0.00	2019-11-09	Sat	3,414.66		956.11		0.00%	8,113.15
2,347.95	0.00	2019-11-10	Sun	1,878.36		525.94		0.00%	8,639.09

(YEAR 2019 MONTH NOV — Mix Total 100.00% — MIX 80.00% — TARGET FOOD 28.00%)

6. After each day, enter the total purchase for each of the category totals in the actually spent column. (This includes all invoices and paid outs.)

Restaurant Checkbook Guardian

YEAR	2019	MONTH	NOV	FOOD					
Mix Total	100.00% Remove Blanks			MIX	80.00%	TARGET	28.00%		
Forecasted Sales	Actual Sales Total	DATE	DAY	Forecasted Food Sales	Actual Food Sales	Food Allotment	Actually Spent	Raw Food Cost %	Estimated Order
4,313.70	3,871.33	2019-11-01	Fri	3,450.96	2,897.33	811.25	125.47	4.33%	685.78
4,268.33	4,512.77	2019-11-02	Sat	3,414.66	3,544.77	992.54	15.23	2.18%	1,663.09
2,347.95	3,351.11	2019-11-03	Sun	1,878.36	3,025.88	847.25		1.49%	2,510.33
2,227.97	4,988.22	2019-11-04	Mon	1,782.38	4,588.01	1,284.64	4,828.99	35.36%	-1,034.01
2,310.80	2,421.31	2019-11-05	Tue	1,848.64	2,045.33	572.69		30.87%	-461.32
2,967.10	0.00	2019-11-06	Wed	2,373.68		664.63		0.00%	203.31
4,418.65	0.00	2019-11-07	Thu	3,534.92		989.78		0.00%	1,193.09
4,313.70	0.00	2019-11-08	Fri	3,450.96		966.27		0.00%	2,159.36
4,268.33	0.00	2019-11-09	Sat	3,414.66		956.11		0.00%	3,115.46
2,347.95	0.00	2019-11-10	Sun	1,878.36		525.94		0.00%	3,641.40
2,227.97	0.00	2019-11-11	Mon	1,782.38		499.07		0.00%	4,140.47
2,310.80	0.00	2019-11-12	Tue	1,848.64		517.62		0.00%	4,658.09

7. When you place your next order, tally up the category allotment column all the way to a specific target delivery date. To get the most out of this system, choose a delivery date that is one day past the order you are about to place. The total allotment will replace what has left the shelves in recent days, plus what will leave the shelves in the future. The goal is to keep working your inventory levels back to your inventory target point.

Restaurant Checkbook Guardian

YEAR	2019	MONTH	NOV	FOOD					
Mix Total	100.00% Remove Blanks			MIX	80.00%	TARGET	28.00%		
Forecasted Sales	Actual Sales Total	DATE	DAY	Forecasted Food Sales	Actual Food Sales	Food Allotment	Actually Spent	Raw Food Cost %	Estimated Order
4,313.70	3,871.33	2019-11-01	Fri	3,450.96	2,897.33	811.25	125.47	4.33%	685.78
4,268.33	4,512.77	2019-11-02	Sat	3,414.66	3,544.77	992.54	15.23	2.18%	1,663.09
2,347.95	3,351.11	2019-11-03	Sun	1,878.36	3,025.88	847.25		1.49%	2,510.33
2,227.97	4,988.22	2019-11-04	Mon	1,782.38	4,588.01	1,284.64	4,828.99	35.36%	-1,034.01
2,310.80	2,421.31	2019-11-05	Tue	1,848.64	2,045.33	572.69		30.87%	-461.32
2,967.10	0.00	2019-11-06	Wed	2,373.68		664.63		0.00%	203.31
4,418.65	0.00	2019-11-07	Thu	3,534.92		989.78		0.00%	1,193.09
4,313.70	0.00	2019-11-08	Fri	3,450.96		966.27		0.00%	2,159.36
4,268.33	0.00	2019-11-09	Sat	3,414.66		956.11		0.00%	3,115.46
2,347.95	0.00	2019-11-10	Sun	1,878.36		525.94		0.00%	3,641.40
2,227.97	0.00	2019-11-11	Mon	1,782.38		499.07		0.00%	4,140.47
2,310.80	0.00	2019-11-12	Tue	1,848.64		517.62		0.00%	4,658.09

The last thing for you to do is subtract the total category actually spent from the total category allotment. This will show how much you can spend on your next order.

The goal is to have controls in place and running so efficiently that you always have enough money to purchase everything you need to operate. If you find that the purchase allotment system isn't indicating enough cash to purchase what you need for an order, then there's a problem somewhere. Once again, you end up with a system that lets you be proactive; you can react immediately to the issue before it gets out of hand.

Now the manager can confidently delegate the task of ordering without being afraid that the bar or kitchen manager will order too much. Set your over/under limit around $250 to $500. If someone needs to spend outside of this window, they must seek your approval.

With this process, you can keep control of your inventory without overloading your shelves or emptying your bank account in the process.

It's critical that you go into the week on budget. You need to know what's going on in your restaurant. You don't have to have your hands in every single thing just to make sure it's done correctly. All you need is the numbers, the right systems, and proper training.

I'm telling you, the purchase allotment system is magic; it's the closest thing that I have to magic. It brings you into the week on budget, no prayers or tears involved. All you need to do is trust your cash controls and remember to ask yourself: What really pays your bills? Cash or profits?

Cash is king.

Think about it. Have you ever had your managers make all your COGS budget targets and still been unable to pay your bills? You may be profitable on paper, but there is no money in the bank account because it's all tied up on your shelves in product that can be easily wasted, spoiled, or stolen.

Cash pays your bills, and profits pay taxes.

CHAPTER TAKEAWAYS

- The key item tracker stops thieves in their tracks.

- The waste tracker isn't meant for a game of NIGYYSOB; it's to help identify opportunities to train your people to be successful.

- The purchase allotment system (Restaurant Checkbook Guardian) removes you from the day to day of your business, giving managers control over everything *except* your checkbook.

CHAPTER 8

MENU ENGINEERING: USING YOUR MENU TO BOOST YOUR PROFITS

I coach so many restaurateurs who have awesome concepts and enough passion to reach the moon, but every day, when they open their doors, they throw their profitability away to dumb-ass luck. They work hard day in and day out and put a lot into what they do to keep their restaurant open, but they're missing two critical systems. These are recipe costing cards and menu engineering. Usually, when I bring up either one of these, the excuses start raining in.

"Oh, David, I don't think that's necessary ... " *It is.*

"But, David, my restaurant is way too busy …" *That's fine. Make time for it.*

Listen, the reality is pretty black and white. Either you work on these systems and start training your people to follow through with them, or you'll just keep bleeding money out.

We're the little guys in this industry. Independents don't have the luxury of skipping over *anything* that can save your bottom line. **Recipe costing cards and menu engineering** are two of the most important systems in any restaurant.

If you needed new tires, do you think you'd walk up to the tire shop to find the manager staring at a stack of tires and thinking, "I don't know what the hell these things cost me … "

He's not going to look you in the eye and say, "Let's just say you give me 125 bucks."

The owner of the tire shop knows *exactly* how much every tire cost him. And he knows exactly what he needs to sell them for if he wants to make money.

Why should your restaurant be any different?

Fixing that issue means you'll need to get your recipe costing cards tamed. I'll go through the process in the next chapter, so just hold off on that for a minute. I want to switch things up and get right into menu engineering because I need you to understand just how important your menu is. By the time we're finished, maybe you'll realize why you need to roll up your sleeves and get in the kitchen.

Back to the lifeblood of your business: the menu.

It's the number one sales tool we use. Think about it. Menus set the tone for everything you do. The menu determines your location, your hours, and the type of decor you choose. Menus tell you who to hire, your demographic, and most importantly, your price point for every item you serve to your guests. If it's done correctly, the menu is your moneymaker.

To be clear, you must have your recipe costing cards completed to go through this process. Without them, the menu engineering process loses some of its steam. Still, if all you have to work with are your key item trackers, waste trackers, and the purchase allotment system, you'll see similar savings even before you sit down to take inventory or get your recipe costing cards mapped out.

I know it's a lot of work, but if you don't get it done, you're robbing yourself. Key item trackers, waste trackers, and the purchase allotment system will leave you looking at a two-to-three-point change even if you don't do anything else. If you follow the instructions in this chapter, menu engineering offers you *another* three to seven points of savings on top of that.

Make two adjustments, and you can reclaim *ten points* to your bottom line. Now do you think it's worth the time?

I'm glad you're starting to come around.

I know there's probably a ton of things you want to fix in your restaurant, things you probably think are more important than this. But even if you're operating with the kitchen from hell, do what you need to do to get on top of recipe costing cards, then work on your menu engineering. It's worth it. You'll recover the points and start banking the savings. It's been proven time and again.

Trust me on this.

No matter what you do, it'll always come back to the menu. Your style of service. Your price point. The quality of your ingredients. The whole environment of your restaurant is determined by what you put on your menu.

I see so many owners planning to open their first restaurant who spend all their time working on these over-the-top architectural plans. They're focused on the restaurant's design and the uniforms and all this other stuff. On paper, their restaurant is beautiful. Then, two weeks before they open, they realize "Oh shit, I need a menu."

It's too late now.

Then there's the group that likes to run their menus on "generals."

They *generally* know what their proteins cost.

They *generally* know what's their best-selling item.

And they *generally* aren't making any money.

The menu is the heart of the business, and its arteries pump cash flow to every other department in your restaurant. It's what pays your bills, pays your staff, and purchases your products. Ultimately, it's the reason why your restaurant turns a profit. If your heart isn't healthy, your arteries are going to get clogged and the body, your restaurant, is going to die off.

Reviewing Your Menu

In one of my speeches, I give an example of a restaurant I really love. The owners are incredible. They're professionals who've been around the block.

Their restaurant's been operating for more than one hundred years out of Buffalo, New York. Before they came to me, things were working well for them. They already had recipe cards in place and a few other systems, but there was still a major issue with their menu that needed to be addressed to be able to survive the fifteen-dollar minimum wage law that was passed in the state of New York.

First of all, there was white-out on the menu for price changes!

How many times have you needed to change a price but didn't

because reprinting your menu would've been too expensive?

What happens when there's an early frost in Florida and the orange crops are destroyed? The price of oranges goes through the roof, and you can say goodbye to whatever you would've profited from selling your hand-squeezed juice, your marmalade, your zest, your citrus salad, or whatever the hell else you can use oranges for.

Without fair warning, you can find 101 reasons to change your menu, and I understand that a lot of independents don't have the budget, the time, or the know-how to reprint. Instead, they go for the quick fix. White-out. Post-its. Permanent marker. Randomly charging new prices at the register. Not when you're using my systems. Not when I'm helping you compete with big chain restaurants. We're going to do this right, or there's no point in doing it at all.

Menu engineering is much more than making sure your options are up to date. It involves proper placement. Understanding what's on each page and how it draws your guests' eyes when they're ordering.

Menu engineering helps you use your menu like a tool to help your restaurant make money. I go into all the nitty-gritty details in my speech. Here, I'll do my best to give you the condensed version.

First, place yourself in your customers' shoes. When you look at your menu, does it make you want to spend money?

What's on it? Is it stamped with all types of crap? You know— watermarks, logos, and anything else people can add to their menu for no reason at all.

What about your font? Listen, I'm in my fifties. I'm supposed to carry around readers wherever I go, but I think my vision is just fine. My optometrist may disagree, but hey, she's not here right now.

The one thing I hate, though, is going into a restaurant and having to hold the menu six feet from my face just to try to see what it says. You know what happens then: the customer doesn't come back. They're embarrassed. Pride kicks in.

Nobody wants to admit there's a problem. Look at me. I'm not carrying glasses with me every time I step outside the house. There are millions of other stubborn restaurant goers in the world. They won't admit something's wrong, and blaming the establishment makes them feel much better.

I always tell restaurant owners, "If it's impossible for you to break up with your logo, at least stick it somewhere in the bottom corner." I'll never understand the relationship we have with logos. I can promise you, nobody's ever looked at a menu and said, "Thank goodness! There's their logo. Now I know where I am ... "

Logos placed in prominent positions on your menu are about ego; nothing more, nothing less.

I don't want you to worry about being a professional right now.

They're there so we can beat our chests and sleep good at night knowing that we're professionals. I don't want you to worry about being a professional right now. I want you to start running your restaurant to make money. That's the only thing that matters.

Menus also help me see where your restaurant is getting bogged down. If you're spending a ton of money at the fry station and it's slowing down your line, let's engineer your menu so a different item catches your guests' eyes.

Look at this "before" menu for a restaurant owner I coached in the past.

"WHERE THE GOOD FOOD IS."

APPETIZERS & STARTERS

NERO'S FAMOUS WHITE BEAN SOUP & CORN CAKES
ORIGINAL RECIPES FROM THE GOOD OLE DAYS
.... **CUP $4.45 • BOWL $5.45**

CHICKEN LETTUCE WRAPS **$9.99**
SPICY CHICKEN TOSSED WITH MUSHROOMS, GREEN ONIONS
AND WATER CHESTNUTS SERVED OVER THAI RICE NOODLES
WITH BIBB LETTUCE

SMOKED SALMON MARTINI **$10.99**
JULIENNE OF WOOD-SMOKED SALMON WITH RED ONION,
CAPERS, EGG AND A CITRUS CHIVE CREAM SAUCE, SERVED
WITH HOMEMADE FRENCH BREAD CROSTINI

SPINACH ARTICHOKE DIP **$8.99**
GREEN HILLS' BEST DIP!! SERVED WITH PARMESAN CROSTINI

HOME-FRIED POTATO CHIPS **$6.99**
TOPPED WITH OUR OWN BLEND OF MELTED BLEU CHEESE

CALAMARI **$8.99**
SERVED WITH A SPICY MARINARA SAUCE

COCONUT SHRIMP **$10.99**
HAND BREADED IN A COCONUT MIXTURE AND SERVED WITH
ORANGE-PINEAPPLE DIPPING SAUCE

MARYLAND STYLE CRAB CAKES.................. **$10.99**
FRESH LUMP CRAB MEAT BLENDED WITH CELERY,
ONIONS AND FRESH HERBS. SERVED WITH OUR
CAJUN REMOULADE SAUCE

BLOODY MARY FRIED OYSTERS **$8.99**
PLUMP OYSTERS DREDGED IN CAJUN SEASONED
CORNMEAL AND SERVED WITH OUR VODKA
COCKTAIL SAUCE

PORTABELLA BRUSCHETTA........................... **$7.99**
TOASTED FOCACCIA BREAD TOPPED WITH BASIL
PESTO, CARAMELIZED ONIONS, MELTED MOZZARELLA
CHEESE AND GARLIC ROASTED PORTABELLAS.
DRIZZLED WITH BALSAMIC CURRANT REDUCTION

SALADS

LETTUCE WEDGE...**$5.99**
A WHOLE BABY ICEBERG HEAD OF LETTUCE SERVED WITH TOMATO, EGG SLICES AND YOUR CHOICE OF DRESSING

WARM SPINACH SALAD...**$7.99**
BABY SPOON SPINACH, RED ONION, BACON BITS, BLEU CHEESE CRUMBLES AND OUR HOMEMADE WARM BACON DRESSING
Add grilled chicken....$4.00 • Add grilled salmon....$5.00 • Add ahi tuna....$8.00

CAESAR SALAD **$6.99**
CRISP HEARTS OF ROMAINE LETTUCE, HOMEMADE CROUTONS, SHREDDED PARMESAN CHEESE AND OUR PEPPERY PARMESAN DRESSING
Add grilled chicken....$4.00 • Add grilled salmon....$5.00 • Add Anchovies....$1.00

COBB SALAD **$11.99**
FRIED OR GRILLED CHICKEN TENDERS ATOP CRISP GREENS, BACON, BLEU CHEESE, EGG AND AVOCADO SERVED WITH YOUR CHOICE OF DRESSING

CHEF SALAD **$9.99**
CRISP GREENS TOPPED WITH JULIENNE SMOKED HAM, TURKEY, JARLSBERG SWISS CHEESE, SLICED EGG, TOMATO, CUCUMBER
AND YOUR CHOICE OF OUR HOMEMADE DRESSING

CRAWFISH AND ASPARAGUS SALAD **$11.99**
MARINATED ASPARAGUS AND CRAWFISH TAIL MEAT WITH FINE DICED PEPPERS, RED ONION AND CILANTRO IN A HONEY
RICE WINE VINAIGRETTE OVER TENDER BIBB LETTUCE

FRESH FRUIT SALAD...SEASONAL
YOUR CHOICE OF OUR HOMEMADE CHICKEN SALAD, OR COTTAGE CHEESE, OR RASPBERRY SORBET SURROUNDED BY SEASONAL FRUIT

SOUP AND SALAD...**$7.99**
YOUR CHOICE OF A CUP OF EITHER OUR WHITE BEAN SOUP OR THE SOUP OF THE DAY ALONG WITH OUR HOUSE SALAD

YOUR CHOICE OF OUR HOMEMADE DRESSINGS:
BALSAMIC VINAIGRETTE, BLEU CHEESE, CAESAR, FAT FREE ITALIAN, HONEY MUSTARD, ITALIAN VINAIGRETTE, PEPPERY BLUEBERRY,
RANCH, THOUSAND ISLAND OR WARM BACON

SANDWICHES AND SUCH

Add a cup of soup to any sandwich **$1.99**

LONE EAGLE **$9.99**
LEGENDARY OPEN FACED SANDWICH WITH SHAVED TURKEY,
HAM AND TOMATO TOPPED WITH PIMENTO CHEESE, THEN
BROILED TO A BUBBLY GOODNESS. SERVED WITH OUR
HOMEMADE COLESLAW

NERO'S ½ LB. CANYON CHEESEBURGER **$8.99**
OR BLACKBEAN BURGER
SERVED WITH OUR TANGY PEPPER SAUCE **Add Bacon....50¢**

CHICKEN SALAD MELT **$8.99**
OPEN FACED ENGLISH MUFFIN WITH OUR HOMEMADE CHICKEN
SALAD TOPPED WITH CHEDDAR CHEESE

PO-BOY SANDWICH **$8.99**
YOUR CHOICE OF OYSTERS OR SHRIMP SERVED ON A HOAGIE
ROLL WITH REMOULADE SAUCE AND ALL THE TRIMMINGS

PULLED PORK BBQ ON CORN CAKES **$9.99**
SERVED WITH OUR HOMEMADE COLESLAW AND YOUR CHOICE
OF SPICY OR MILD SAUCE

GRILLED CHICKEN SANDWICH **$8.99**
JUICY 8 OZ. MARINATED BREAST SERVED WITH RED ONION,
LETTUCE, TOMATO AND PICKLE **Add Blackened....50¢**

TRADITIONAL FIVE LAYER CLUB **$9.99**
THREE LAYERS PILED HIGH WITH BACON, LETTUCE, TOMATO,
SWISS CHEESE, HAM, TURKEY AND MAYONNAISE WITH
CHOICE OF WHITE OR WHEAT BREAD

CHICKEN SALAD CROISSANT **$8.99**
A FRESHLY BAKED CROISSANT PILED HIGH WITH OUR
HOMEMADE CHICKEN SALAD

BUFFALO CHICKEN WRAP **$9.99**
FRIED CHICKEN TENDERS TOSSED IN OUR BUFFALO SAUCE,
LETTUCE, TOMATO, PICKLE AND CHIPOTLE MAYO, WRAPPED
IN A SPINACH TORTILLA

VEGETABLE WRAP **$8.99**
CRISP LETTUCE, TOMATOES, ZUCCHINI, CUCUMBER, ROASTED
RED PEPPER AND SPICY SPROUTS WRAPPED IN A SPINACH
TORTILLA AND SERVED WITH LIME CHIPOTLE MAYONNAISE
Add Grilled Chicken....$4.00

GRILLED SALMON CLUB **$13.99**
A HONEY GLAZED FILLET TOPPED WITH BACON, YOUR CHOICE OF CHEESE

SKINNY NERO **$8.99**
YOUR CHOICE OF OUR BURGER OR CHICKEN BREAST, NO BUN, ALL THE
TRIMMINGS WITH CHOICE OF COTTAGE CHEESE OR FRUIT

ENTREES

Add House Salad **$3.99**

STEAK AND BISCUITS **$10.99**
TENDER, JUICY PAN SEARED MEDALLIONS OF BEEF INSIDE
THREE FLAKY BUTTERMILK BISCUITS. SERVED WITH
COLESLAW AND FRENCH FRIES

GRILLED ELK TENDERLOIN **$17.99**
PEPPERCORN CRUSTED AND WOOD GRILLED, SERVED
WITH CHEF'S VEGETABLES AND YOUR CHOICE OF POTATO

GRILLED LEMON CHICKEN **$13.99**
GRILLED BREAST TOPPED WITH A CITRUS MUSHROOM
ARTICHOKE SAUCE. SERVED WITH CHEF'S VEGETABLES AND
CALICO RICE

CRUNCHY TROUT **$12.99**
FRITO ENCRUSTED, SAUTEED AND FINISHED WITH A CILANTRO
LIME TEQUILA DRIZZLE, AVOCADO, TOMATO SALSA AND A BLACK
BEAN CORN RELISH **Add an Extra Fillet....$5.00**

CAJUN BOW TIE PASTA **$13.99**
CRAWFISH, ANDOUILLE SAUSAGE, MUSHROOM, ASPARAGUS,
BLACK BEANS, YELLOW CORN AND OKRA PAN TOSSED IN
A CAJUN CREAM SAUCE

NEW YORK STRIP **$16.99**
10 OZ. CUT GRILLED OVER HICKORY AND SERVED WITH CHEF'S
VEGETABLES AND YOUR CHOICE OF POTATO

AHI TUNA **$15.99**
CAJUN SILICAR SEARED, SERVED ON A SET OF SPINACH WITH
SESAME SEAWEED SALAD, PICKLED GINGER, WASABI AND
SWEET SOY DRIZZLE

BBQ HALF CHICKEN **$12.99**
A ROASTED HALF CHICKEN BRUSHED WITH OUR SPECIAL BBQ
SAUCE AND GRILLED OVER HICKORY WOOD. SERVED WITH
HOMEMADE COLESLAW AND FRENCH FRIES

PENNE PASTA PRIMAVERA **$9.99**
PAN TOSSED WITH AN ARRAY OF VEGETABLES IN A CREAMY
PARMESAN CHEESE SAUCE
Add Chicken....$4.00 • Add Shrimp....$5.00

BO'S PASTA **$9.99**
PENNE PASTA TOSSED WITH OUR MARINARA SAUCE AND
TOPPED WITH FRESH PARMESAN CHEESE
Add Chicken....$4.00 • Add Shrimp....$5.00

VEGGIE PLATE **$10.99**
GRILLED PORTOBELLO MUSHROOM, SAUTEED SPINACH,
ASPARAGUS, AND CHEF VEGETABLE MEDLEY

CHICKEN QUESADILLA **$9.99**
A BIG FLOUR TORTILLA FILLED WITH BLACK BEANS & CORN, VEGGIES,
CHEESE, & GRILLED CHICKEN BREAST. SERVED WITH SALSA & SOUR CREAM

▼ MARKS OUR SIGNATURE ITEMS
ALL SANDWICHES SERVED WITH YOUR CHOICE OF HOME FRIED POTATO CHIPS OR FRENCH FRIES
DESSERT MENU AVAILABLE UPON REQUEST / SPLIT PLATE CHARGE $2.00
2122 HILLSBORO DRIVE • NASHVILLE, TENNESSEE 37215 • 615.297.7777 • WWW.NEROSGRILL.COM
KEEP US IN MIND FOR YOUR NEXT PRIVATE PARTY OR GET-TOGETHER!

Do you see where "Maryland Style Crab Cakes" are on the menu?

OK, take a look at this "after" design. Tell me where your eyes are drawn.

Appetizers

NERO'S GRILL

Gun Powder Onions
Thinly sliced onion strings
dusted in a spicy batter and served
with Cajun Remoulade Sauce. 6.99

Maryland Style Crab Cakes
Fresh lump crab meat blended with celery,
onions and fresh herbs. Served with our
Cajun Remoulade sauce. 12.99

Nero's Famous White Bean Soup
CUP 4.99 ✤ BOWL 5.99

Calamari
Tossed in our spicy seasoning mix
and fried to a golden crisp. Served
with zesty marinara sauce. 9.99

Hand Sliced Chips
Topped with Bleu cheese crumbles
and served with warm
Bleu cheese sauce. 6.99

Spinach Artichoke Dip
Green Hills' best dip!! Served with
Parmesan crostini. 9.99

Entrées
All Grilled Items are prepared over a hickory wood flame. Add a house salad 3.99

Ahi Tuna
Cajun sugar seared, served on a
bed of spinach with sesame seaweed
salad, pickled ginger, wasabi and
a sweet soy drizzle. 15.99

Chicken Quesadilla
A large flour tortilla filled with
grilled chicken, black beans & corn,
veggies, and cheese. Served with
salsa and sour cream. 10.99

Crunchy Trout
Frito encrusted sautéed and
finished with a cilantro lime
tequila drizzle, avocado, tomato
salsa and a black bean
corn relish. 12.99
ADD AN EXTRA FILET 5.00

Veggie Plate
Sautéed mushrooms, steamed
broccoli, fresh spinach and steamed
seasonal vegetables. 10.99

Cajun Bowtie Pasta
Crawfish, andouille sausage,
mushroom, asparagus, black beans,
yellow corn and okra pan tossed in a
Cajun cream sauce. 13.99

Grilled Lemon Chicken
Grilled chicken breast topped
with a citrus mushroom
artichoke sauce, served with
a vegetable medley and
calico rice. 13.99

Skinny Nero
Your choice of our burger or chicken
breast, no bun, all the trimmings and
cottage cheese or fresh fruit. 10.99

Strawberry Tilapia
Grilled Tilapia topped with a
strawberry salsa served with steamed
seasonal vegetable. 13.99

Sandwiches
Served with your choice of Hand Sliced Chips or French Fries.
Add a cup of soup 2.99

Lone Eagle
Legendary open faced sandwich
with shaved turkey, ham and
tomato topped with pimento
cheese then broiled to a
bubbly goodness. 11.99

Traditional Three Layer Club
Three layers piled high with bacon,
lettuce, tomato, Swiss cheese,
ham, turkey and mayonnaise on
your choice of toasted wheat
or white bread. 9.99

Rib Rolls
Shaved prime rib with melted
provolone cheese inside three Sister
Schubert rolls. 12.99

Pulled Pork BBQ
Hand pulled BBQ pork served atop
our famous corn cakes. 9.99

Chicken Salad Melt
Open faced English muffin with
our chicken salad topped with
cheddar cheese. 9.99

**Green Hills Best Burger or
Seasoned Black Bean Burger**
½ pound of lean ground beef
seasoned and grilled to your
liking. 9.99
ADD CHEESE .50 ✤ ADD BACON .50

Chicken Salad Croissant
A freshly baked croissant piled high
with chicken salad. 8.99

Grilled Chicken Sandwich
A juicy marinated chicken breast
grilled to perfection and served
with red onion, lettuce and
pickle. 10.99 BLACKENED ADD .50

Steak and Biscuits
Tender, juicy pan seared
medallions of beef inside three
flaky buttermilk biscuits. 12.99

Buffalo Chicken Wrap
Fried or grilled chicken tenders tossed
in our homemade sauce, lettuce,
tomato, pickle and chipotle mayo,
wrapped in a spinach tortilla. 10.99

Salads
Our dressings: Creamy Balsamic, Bleu Cheese, Honey Mustard, Italian Vinaigrette,
Ranch, Fat Free Raspberry Vinaigrette or Warm Bacon

Black 'n Bleu
Steak medallions over crisp spring
mix lettuce and tossed in a creamy
balsamic vinaigrette. Topped with
pine nuts, bleu cheese crumbles
and red onions. 13.99

Lettuce Wedge
A baby iceberg head of lettuce served
with tomato, egg slices and your
choice of dressing. 5.99

Cobb Salad
Fried or grilled chicken atop
crisp greens, tomatoes, bacon,
bleu cheese, egg and avocado.
Served with your choice of
dressing. 11.99

Lunch Combo
Your choice of two: Cup of Soup,
Baked Potato, Stuffed Potato, House
or Caesar Salad. 8.99

Caesar Salad
Crisp hearts of Romaine lettuce,
seasoned croutons, shredded
Parmesan cheese and tossed in
our Caesar dressing. 6.99
ADD GRILLED CHICKEN 4.00
ADD GRILLED SALMON 6.00
ADD AHI TUNA 8.00

Warm Spinach Salad
Baby Spoon Spinach, red onion,
bacon bits, bleu cheese crumbles and
our warm bacon dressing. 7.99
ADD GRILLED CHICKEN 4.00
ADD GRILLED SALMON 6.00
ADD AHI TUNA 8.00

Chop Chop
Italian inspired salad of
shredded iceburg lettuce,
smoked turkey, provolone cheese,
diced tomatoes, artichokes,
chick peas, scallions, fresh basil
and croutons all tossed in our
Italian vinaigrette. 11.99

Split plate charge 2.00.   20% Gratuity added to parties of 6 or more.
An additional .50 will be added to all carry-out orders.
2122 Hillsboro Drive • Nashville, Tennessee 37215 • 615-297-7777 • www.NerosGrill.com

Not only does this new menu control where the guests' attention is concentrated but we've also raised the price of those crab cakes, one of the restaurant's best-selling items, to $12.99.

Do you think the recipe cost jumped two bucks overnight? Absolutely not. The only thing that changed was the fact that we engineered their menu to bring more attention to that plate.

Nobody cared about the fact that the price went up. Sales didn't drop. As a matter of fact, the sales went through the roof!

Before we stepped in, they weren't charging enough for that product. It was the most delicious, full-on lump crab meat you could find. No fillers. Top-quality product. They just weren't getting the money they deserved for it.

But we fixed that problem for them. Then the benefits started pouring in.

Food costs went down. Profits went up. Labor costs dropped, too, but that's another story.

That's how you properly engineer a menu to start working in your favor. By the time you're done, everything starts shifting so cash can keep flowing through your business like it should've been from the beginning.

How to Start Engineering Your Menu

The menu engineering process starts with accurate, up-to-date recipe costing cards and your menu mix from your POS system. We'll go into this even more in the next chapter.

When we work through the step-by-step process of engineering a menu, we pay attention to every detail. Here are ten key things to focus on when evaluating your menu.

1—Eye movement. That's the biggest thing we changed with this earlier example. You can see it's a lunch menu, and normally that would mean appetizers followed by soups and salads stamped across the top of the page, then sandwiches and entrées. But who said that was the only way to do things?

With this restaurant, we chose to target key items that would make the most money.

We dropped salads off to the bottom of the page. Why? We don't need to promote them in prime eye movement real estate (which is the top half of the menu) on a single-panel menu.

Plus, I've got news for you: the rabbits will find their food!

Think about it.

Whoever's interested in eating a salad for lunch will find the salads, wherever they are. They don't need you to market salad to them. There's no benefit in placing so much emphasis on salads because you don't make a lot of money on them. They slow down the kitchen. The staff hates making them.

Let the salad sell itself, and concentrate on making more money. Promote your entrées and appetizers instead.

And don't be scared to raise your prices. Some people will hold on to the same prices for two or three years because they're scared of losing customers. Does losing *money* on every fricking customer who walks in the door seem like a better solution?

> **Believe it or not, the only person who has a problem with your prices is you.**

Believe it or not, the only person who has a problem with your prices is you. I want you to profit confidently. I don't need you adding a dollar to a plate, then hunkering down like you were in the middle of a war. I don't want to see you somewhere peeking over the counter and waiting for a sniper to put one right between your eyes because you're scared of getting a little pushback from your customers.

People pay for what they want. Sure, you may get a little huff and puff from the old-timer that loves coming to your diner for breakfast every morning, but after they've said their piece, they're going to place their order. It happens time and again.

2—Ambiance. Does everything about your restaurant make sense? I've seen high-end steak houses with ratty insert plastic menus with rusting tabs and loose threads. But you want to charge me fifty dollars a plate? You've got to be kidding.

I've also seen casual concepts with prices along the lines of your average Applebee's and Chili's, but they've got these custom wooden menu covers with laser-etched logos and leather binding. It does something to the psychology of the customer's mind and makes them think you're an expensive restaurant.

The prices may not be high, but the menu tells me that it is. Even though it isn't expensive, guest perception will tell the customer they can't come back that often because your restaurant's out of their budget.

3—Demographic. Make sure your menu's telling your guests that you sell what they want. Give your neighborhood what they need. Either that or move to a neighborhood with a demographic that makes sense. You're going to have a real challenge making money showcasing a gourmet chef and a menu featuring French cuisine in the middle of farm country.

Everything must flow naturally. Minimize the resistance so your restaurant can take off and the money can start raining in.

4—Pricing. Fine dining owners can skip this section since it won't apply to you. I mean, what the hell is the difference between $34 and $35?

A dollar, right? Your customers will still buy the item without thinking about it.

If you're selling an item for $10.00 but the price of beef just went through the roof, you still need to buy beef. Raising your price to $10.25 isn't going to kill anyone, nor will your customers notice the change. These incremental adjustments give you enough room to make three more price changes before you go over the $11.00 barrier: $10.50, $10.75, and $10.95.

Engineering your menu the right way may mean you only have to raise the price on your top two or three sellers in each section. This way, you can earn the cash you need without having to shock your guests by skyrocketing the whole menu.

5—Cash contribution. If I have a steak house, I'm expected to have higher food costs. Even with the higher numbers, I can still come in at 55 percent prime cost—or even lower.

Let's look at a breakdown:

You sell a cheeseburger at $5.50.

Cost to you is $1.13.

Remember the equation? **use ÷ sales** = 20.55 percent

$$\$5.50 - \$1.13 = \$4.37$$

That's your contribution margin, otherwise known as cash contribution. When you subtract the cost of an item from your menu price, you'll come up with how much money you make on the item. Just remember, you don't take profits to the bank, you take cash.

I can give you another example. It's thirteen years old, so don't laugh at my numbers—just stick with me until I prove my point.

You're selling steak for $12.95. (I said don't laugh!)

It's the exact same steak as the one being sold at the steak house down the street, but for some reason, nobody in your sports bar is buying it. Why?

Because perception is everything.

You're the only one sitting at the bar tearing into this juicy T-bone steak because no one else understands why you're selling it for so low. To them, it must be a piece of crap at the price, so they'll never give it a try.

Often, the price you list your products for tells your audience what it's worth.

Note: If you can't charge what the product is worth, it doesn't belong on your menu.

You sell the T-bone for $12.95.

Cost to you is $5.50.

$$\textbf{use} \div \textbf{sales} = 42.47 \text{ percent}$$
$$\$12.95 - \$5.50 = \$7.45$$

You make $7.45 each time you sell this item.

With the numbers in hand, which should you sell: the burger or the steak?

The answer ultimately depends on what you set as your target food cost in your budget.

If you want lower food costs, then sell the burger. If you know you won't sell too many steaks but you want your prime cost to drop, then sell the heck out of the T-bone on your menu.

You're paying your cook $15.00 per hour whether he's flipping burgers or dropping steaks on the grill. If you're selling one item for more than twice the price of the other at the register, even with a higher COGS, it's bringing your restaurant a greater cash contribution.

At the same time, it's lowering your labor costs and benefiting your prime cost.

(Remember, you can't see these savings or profit if you don't have good recipe costing cards. Don't worry, we're almost to that part.)

6—Menu descriptions. Fine dining, this may not be one for you either. Still, it's worth a quick read.

So you serve duck confit and rice pilaf or whatever fancy plates you've put on your menu. Those don't really need a heavy description. Let the dish speak for itself.

On the other hand, casual concept restaurants should sell a little more detail in their menu descriptions.

OK, your menu says you sell a chicken breast sandwich. Then you tell your guest they'll be getting chicken breast, a sesame seed bun, lettuce, tomato, mayo, and provolone cheese.

Are you shitting me?

That's a damn grocery list.

You just told me how to go home and make it myself—and reminded me that it'd probably be a lot cheaper if I did. Now your restaurant's useless to me.

I'm eating out for an experience. To get something tempting and appetizing. Wouldn't you rather go out and see a "teriyaki chicken burger" on the menu? Something with a description like "Savory grilled chicken breast brushed with a sweet teriyaki sauce and topped with Hawaiian pineapple and melted cheddar …"

I sure as hell would!

The point is make sure your menu's selling items that sound like they're worth your guests' money. That's what makes your restaurant attractive.

7—Fonts. Keep it as simple as possible. Don't assault the guests' eyes with more than three fonts on the menu. This isn't the eighties, and you're not a preteen who just discovered a new website with thousands of free fonts and clip art. The menu is a sales tool. You want your guests to stay focused on the task at hand. Choose a font that's easy to read. I like sans serif fonts, such as Tahoma or Helvetica, for category headers and menu items. And for menu description a serif font like Times Roman.

8—Price lists. Death to them all. Forget about the fricking price list. If I see another, I'm going to choke someone.

Price lists don't do anything but help your customer figure out how to keep their money in their wallets. It tells them to stay away from the best item on the menu because it's the most expensive. It turns them into price shoppers.

Let's look at that menu example again.

See that long row of dots leading to the price for each appetizer and starter? If I had hair, I'd pull it out every time I saw one of those.

These itemized price lists train the guest to evaluate your menu on everything besides how great these plates probably taste. You want guys like me in your restaurant. I'm coming in for a good meal. I'm not looking for prices. I want something that sounds delicious when I read the description, but price lists instantly change my train of thought. Now you've brought cost to my attention.

When budget shoppers are dining in your restaurant, these lists teach them to scan for the least expensive item. That doesn't help your restaurant make money.

The price list has got to go!

Studies show that if a menu has five items side by side, the first, second, and last will sell the most.[2] I'll probably see the same thing if I looked at your sales mix report. Usually, the only exception to the rule is restaurants with a signature item in that section—those sell no matter where they are placed.

If you want to make more money, you need to engineer your menu to appeal to the customer's psychology, letting the recipe costing cards be your guide.

9—White space. An absolute necessity. Since I'm throwing out statistics, I may as well share that studies also show that 50 percent of your menu should be white space.

I know it probably sounds like a nightmare for owners who've crammed every picture, description, font, and special offer they could fit onto a page.

For the record, 50 percent white space doesn't mean order bigger paper, OK?

It means reducing the number of items you sell. It means understanding your product mix. It means using what we know about merchandising to create your menu.

It's a sales tool, remember?

10—Pictures. While pictures are not appropriate for all restaurants, know that pictures sell!

Please make sure you use good ones. Back in my restaurant days, I may have found myself slouched over drunk in Denny's at two in the morning, looking cross-eyed at the menu and pointing at the pretty picture to order.

Have you ever wondered why they have pictures? Well, it's not for the drunks, contrary to popular belief. It's because pictures influence the guest to order that item. It's sales psychology.

---

2   All data in this chapter are drawn from Jack E. Miller and David V. Pavesic, *Menu: Pricing & Strategy* (Wiley, 1996).

Don't just add any picture—use pictures of items that are, first and foremost, great items. Next, you should know that whatever item you use will fly off the shelves.

Be careful not to overdo it either. Think two, maybe three, pictures per page. That should do.

Keep Engineering

You need to push the envelope. If you don't, you'll never know your limits. Use customer response to continue engineering your menu.

Remember, nothing's ever set in stone. That goes for every part of your business. At the same time, I need you to understand that you can't be all things to all people.

I don't care what's happening in your market. You won't be able to keep up with the Joneses all the time.

If you're a casual concept restaurant, and down the street, somebody opens a steak house, don't add steaks to your menu out of the blue.

If a new breakfast spot opens around the corner, don't pop up with a brand-new breakfast menu.

If someone decides to put a Mexican food restaurant two doors down, you don't need to add Mexican dishes to your menu.

Be true to yourself. That's how you'll make the best impression on your guests.

Chains such as In-N-Out Burger and Chipotle succeed because they stay true to what they know. Hell, Chipotle has like four items on the menu. They switch things up and serve them five different ways. And people keep the lines out the door.

The perfect menu has ten items that sell 10 percent each. Unfortunately, that's never going to happen.

For most restaurant owners, I tell them to target thirty-five menu items, including appetizers and desserts.

I hear you sports bar owners. "There's no way in hell I can do that, David!" For you, I'm aiming for closer to sixty-five items.

You read that correctly.

Know that your menu will go through routine changes. You'll always add, remove, and change items around. With that in mind, I often say, "Death to the laminated menu!"

People look at laminated menus like they're unchangeable. You can laminate if you want. You just need to know that if the cost of tomatoes blows up, you need to have a plan to take them off your menu or change your pricing. Crazy how a single ingredient can change *everything* about your business, isn't it?

It comes back around to your recipe cards. I think this is the perfect time to dive right into that painstaking—but oh so necessary—process. Let's get to it in the next chapter.

CHAPTER TAKEAWAYS

- The menu sets the tone for everything in your restaurant; don't let it be the last thing you do.

- Recipe costing cards are not optional. You need to invest the man hours required to get them done.

- Menu engineering is an ongoing process. That's why I think laminated menus suck. Use customer response to continue to tweak your menu so that it makes people want to spend money.

CHAPTER 9

UNDERSTANDING THE RECIPE COSTING CARD PROCESS

You already know that I can't cook. I have zero knife skills.

It's horrible. You don't want to see it.

But I didn't become the expert by knowing how to sear a steak to perfection. I'm the expert because I learned to master the systems that can run any kitchen anywhere in the world.

In the last chapter, I stressed the fact that menu engineering and recipe costing are two systems that can save your restaurant from drowning in a sea of debt. Now it's time to prove it.

I told you in chapter 6 that two of the most important systems in your restaurant are budgets and recipe costing cards. When I go out to work with my owners, what are the two most common systems they never have? You guessed it—budgets and recipe costing cards.

You're probably asking yourself why. Why does everything fall on the menu so heavily?

If you want the most basic answer, I'd just say it's cost control. You've got to know what everything is costing you in order to have a chance to make money.

If you want to dive a little deeper, we'd start talking about things like consistency and creating a standard for the experience you're offering everyone who visits (or works in) your business.

We all know that many chain restaurants suck, but they stay busy because they suck the same way every single time you visit. Their doors stay open, and they keep on franchising because they've placed special attention on the basics of restaurant operation, the stuff that most independents miss.

Systems like menu engineering and recipe costing cards help the fat suits sitting in the corporate office understand everything they need to know to run the business on hard numbers, not "general" assumptions.

Let's walk through the recipe costing card process so you can map out exactly what you should be doing to completely renovate the way you run your business.

The Basic Recipe Costing Card Process

A lot of owners find themselves stuck in this unhealthy comfort zone created by "the old way." Armed with paper, pencil, and a calculator, they do their best to compute their recipe costs by going through a long, drawn-out process complete with lots of guesstimates and even more mistakes. Today, I'm going to show you why the old way is considered old for a reason.

Here's a hint: *systems*.

First things first, stop letting the chef pull out prices from the crack of his or her butt.

Look at the menu. How did you come up with your prices? Most of time, the conversation goes something like this:

"Hey, Chef! How much is this special?"

"I don't know. What did we charge yesterday?"

"$13.95?"

The chef stares at the plate and says, "OK, let's just go with that again."

That's ridiculous.

I need you to set aside forty to sixty man hours to get this done right. Don't bitch about it. A couple of hours of attention to make sure you're working with a properly engineered menu and accurate recipe costing cards spills over to every area of your operation that's costing you too much money. It means you'll start taking better inventory and more money will start coming into (and *staying* in) your restaurant.

This is why you can't really complete your menu engineering without the recipe costing cards. The only way you can truly understand how to position your menu—what items should be highlighted, which to remove, what prices to raise or portion sizes to change—is by completing your recipe costing cards.

Now that you're committed to doing this, let's dive right in.

Here's a short list of what you need to gather to start your recipe costing cards:

- cook's name,

- recipe name,

- date,

- recipe yield (that's for your batch recipes, which we'll get to in a minute),

- ingredients (your shopping list),

- product cost (the cost of how you purchase it),

- quantity (what's in the total order when you get it from the vendor),

- product yield (this requires routine yield tests), and

- recipe quantity (we may cook by the cup, but we cost by the ounce, gram, or per each item).

You'll find a sample recipe costing card on the next page. Here's the simplified recipe costing card process that usually goes along with it.

1. In column E, list all the ingredients that will be used in the recipe.

2. In column A, write in the price of the ingredient as it appears on the vendor invoice.

3. Convert how the ingredient is shipped into ounces, and write the number of ounces in column B.

4. Next, you must complete a yield test on each ingredient. I'll walk you through this process in just a moment.

5. Next, to find the number of usable ounces, multiply column B with column C, and write that answer in column D.

6. In column F, write in the number of ounces of each ingredient you will be using in this recipe.

7. Next, divide column A by column D to get the price per usable ounce, and write it in column G.

8. Now multiply column F by column G to get the total cost of each ingredient used in the recipe.

9. Now total up column H at the bottom in box I.

10. In box J, write in the target food cost percentage you are shooting for.

11. Now take the total item cost in box I and divide that number by the food cost percentage in box J, and write that answer in box K. This number will be a suggested selling price for the item.

12. Finally, review the suggested selling price, and determine if the item as it is costed out is salable. If it is not, due to the price being too high, either change the amount of the ingredients used in the recipe or scrap the idea. If it is determined that the item is salable, come up with a final item sales price based on what the market will bear.

RECIPE COSTING CARD

Cook's Name ————————————————   Date ————————————

Recipe Name ————————————————   Yield ————————————

A COST	B QTY.	C YIELD TEST PERCENT	D QTY. IN USABLE OZ.	E INGREDIENTS	F RECIPE QTY.	G PRICE PER OZ.	H TOTAL AMOUNT
	I		TOTAL COST				
	J		TARGET FC %				
	K		TARGET PRICE				

That seems really easy. And the truth is the process *is* easy. The only reason why recipe costing cards are so hard to complete is because they are extremely time consuming.

To ensure your recipe costing cards are accurate, you have to consider the following.

Yield tests. Do you know what they are?

They tell you the amount of *usable product* you get out of every ingredient you order.

If you get a case of heads of romaine lettuce in the restaurant, you're never going to use it all. Your *product yield* is only how much of the product is useable. Don't count the product that you throw away.

Despite the apprehension around this process, calculating yield could be one of the easiest things you do in your restaurant—you just need to know how to do it the right way.

This means that you need to weigh your product twice to be accurate.

The yield test **divides the ending weight by the beginning weight** of that case—and that's where you get your yield percentage.

Here's a simple example: grab a head of romaine and lay it out on the cutting board. Chop off the top end of the leaves. They're wilted, brown, and have worms crawling all around. You can't serve it, so you throw it away. Then you hack off the bottom end. It's like an apple core, only a goat would eat it. I can't cook, but I know that if I paid ten cents an ounce for that romaine and, with my poor knife skills, I end up tossing 50 percent of it in the trash, the romaine I can use in my salads is actually worth twenty cents per usable ounce.

I paid for 100 percent of the product, whether I use it or not. Weighing the product twice makes a big difference in determining your food costs. And it means a lot to your bottom line.

Too many chefs and kitchen managers use the starting ten cents an ounce in their recipe costing cards, which makes them incredibly inaccurate and undervalued.

It throws everything off.

You've got to do the same thing with your meats too. You paid XYZ for your beef, but that includes the fat you trim and the blood hanging around in the bottom of the bag. Throwing it away doesn't change the fact that it's already come out of your pocket.

What's left doesn't magically become worth more money. Again, you have to write down the starting weight of the product, butcher it, and weigh it again.

Can you see why this is so important? When you do them correctly, your recipe costing cards will reflect the fact that you always pay *more* per usable ounce than whatever's on the invoice.

You need to do this quarterly to get an accurate understanding of how your product yield changes on a routine basis. Things will fluctuate based on two major factors: (1) how the product comes to you from your distributor and (2) how your kitchen team handles that product. Both can have a dramatic effect on your costing.

It's not just products you take a knife to that need yield tests completed to know the actual usable ounce or "each cost." Take chicken wings, for example. You purchase chicken wings by the pound, but you use them wing by wing.

You have to take five cases and count how many come in a forty-pound case to come up with an average count. Divide the price of the case by the average count, and you will come up with the cost per wing or each cost.

This is another exercise you need to perform quarterly. Think about it. What happens each summer? Chickens are anorexic, and it takes more chicken wings to fill the forty-pound case! So your count will go up.

Why does this even matter? Because it's impossible to create accurate recipe costing cards if you don't understand your ingredients.

To be honest, we're kind of jumping in too fast because no recipe costing card is complete without batch recipes. But we'll get to those in a second.

Right now, I'm going to walk you through what you need to do to get both completed; this is the process that needs to be repeated for every single item on your menu.

Once upon a time, I found this book called *The Book of Yields*.[3] It's not restaurant specific, but it does list out product yields for an encyclopedic number of products. And for restaurants that need to get started on recipe costing cards but don't have the time to create their own yields, it's a great place to begin. Ultimately, it helped me appreciate the next point I'm about to bring up.

You need to know what kind of knife skills you have hacking away at your money—I mean, ingredients.

I coached one restaurant owner who owns a $2 million sandwich shop in California. He sells so many damn sandwiches that he's figured out how to walk away with a 100 percent yield on tomatoes. In his kitchen, they slice tomatoes for the sandwiches, then use all the ends and the core to make homemade tomato basil soup. Pure genius!

Then another restaurant owner who barely sells any sandwiches and cores and throws away the ends of their tomatoes maybe gets an 85 percent yield of usable product.

If you had me in your kitchen, I'm telling you, you'd be in the negative. Let's just be real.

That's why calculating your own yields is much more accurate

---

3   Francis T. Lynch, *The Book of Yields: Accuracy in Food Costing and Purchasing*, 8th ed. (John Wiley and Sons, 2010).

than what you can find in any book. You need to know what your kitchen team's knife skills are and how they utilize your products in your restaurant. Period. There's no way around it, not if you want accurate recipe costing cards to work with.

Add the Spice or Consumable Factor

If you've followed all my directions so far, your recipe cards will still be wrong.

"What, David? You just had me walk through all these steps—what do you mean it's still wrong?"

Going through the basics barely scratches the surface of how you're using your products. We talked about the difference yield tests can make on your recipe costing cards. Now I want you to think about all the things you give away for free.

That bread and butter or chips and salsa you put out on the table for starters.

The condiments sitting on your table. Salt. Pepper. Ketchup. Sugar.

It's free to the guest, but it's costing you money. And if you use more product and don't bring in sales for them, what are you doing? You're making your actual food cost go up!

Personally, I don't give anything away for free.

No, I'm not telling you to walk up to table 22 and say, "Oh, excuse me, it looks like you've used about thirty-five cents of mustard. Let me add that to your check."

Just wait until Yelp gets a hold of that son of a bitch—you'd be freakin' dead, man!

What I am suggesting, however, is that you start accounting for these things when you're calculating your food cost and your inventory.

Take inventory of all the products you give away for free. You need a detailed list of everything you prep or purchase and don't charge for. That means if you're making your own salsa, you need to know the dollar value for it.

The calculation for beginning inventory is

beginning inventory + purchases – ending = use

"Use" is simply how much money left the shelves.

Take the beginning inventory of everything prepped or purchased that you give away for free. Add up all your purchases and/or what you prepped of those items between the beginning and ending inventory of those items. At the end of the period—the month, the week, whenever you're taking inventory for value—you need to take an inventory of what's been given away for free.

use = how much product actually left the shelves for free

When you know what left your shelves by dollar value, head over to that expensive cash register called the POS system. Run an item-by-item sales mix report or velocity report or PLU report. I don't care what you call it: you need to know how many entrées (only) you sold during that period.

# of entrées ÷ dollar value of product given away for free = spice factor

The spice factor or consumable factor could be $0.35, $0.25, or $1.65. Whatever you come up with must now become an ingredient on every item recipe that is for an entrée. Now, when you price your entrées, you aren't giving away products for free. You're charging for them with every entrée sold, which covers the cost for purchasing them.

That is a game changer.

You may need to do the same thing for the oils you use in your fryers. It's food. It's inventory. It's costing you money, and it's a required component to get these items on the menu. Why isn't it on your recipe costing cards for all your fried items then?

Following the same process, it's the dollar value of all the oil you used during that period divided by the number of fried menu items you sold. Now you have a fryer oil factor that gets added to all fried items sold.

Restaurant owners give away too much product for free, and that's the reason why their food cost seems so impossible to manage.

When to Add Paper

Now let's get into paper products. Here's another ingredient most people miss.

"What do you mean 'ingredient'? People don't eat paper, David."

If you're using paper 100 percent of the time with a menu item, it's a menu ingredient that needs to be accounted for in the recipe costing card.

If I'm running a taco truck and I sell and wrap each one of my tacos in parchment paper—I mean, there's no other way to serve them, no plates, no cups, nothing but parchment paper—then 100 percent of the time, that paper is food. If you buy it as food and use it as an ingredient, then it needs to be in the recipe.

On the other hand, if you're running a pizza place, boxes should not be in the recipe unless you sell them 100 percent to go. If a pizza box is only used when the pizza is to go, when it comes to calculating food cost on the recipe costing costs, you can't add it. If you do, you're only padding your numbers with to-go costs that aren't actually ingredients. When you actually hit your food cost target, you'll think you're good, but in reality, you've wasted money because you falsely inflated your usage.

If your numbers are padded, when you calculate your ideal food cost, it'll look like you really used the dollar value of a box for every pizza sold when you only used them half of the time. So that means if you hit your target you're actually overusing other ingredients that equaled the dollar value of the pizza boxes that the calculation thought you were using the whole time.

In short, paper is only a part of the recipe card if it's used 100 percent of the time. If it's not, then it's just a paper expense.

Batch Item Recipes

Now you've got your yield tests done. You've figured out your spice factor, and you've worked in paper goods on the recipe costing cards. There's one more thing to work on, and it's major!

You gotta complete your batch recipes.

Batch recipes are those items you make/manufacture in house like soups, sauces, side dishes, dressings, and desserts. From croutons to house-made juices and syrups, they're anything you make from scratch that's on your menu. Another way to look at batch items is they are any component or ingredient you make or prep for any dishes you sell.

Go ahead and grab your menu now. Start at the top and work your way down. Look at every item you sell, then make a list of the ingredients that are made in house for that item.

For example, let's go back to chicken wings. How many people serve wings in their restaurant? When converting a forty-pound case of wings to an each price, you need to think about batch recipes. Those carrots and celery sticks that nobody ever eats—don't know why people still put them on the plate—those need to be batch recipes. The barbecue sauce, buffalo sauce, and blue cheese dressing—if it's something you're whipping up in the kitchen, you need the batch recipe.

Just like I said when we were covering checklists, no detail is too small. Batch recipes can really eat away at your profits. I need you to *make the time* if you can't find it. Batch recipes are that important.

If you don't feel like your managers will document your batch recipes, then you need to stand your ass in the kitchen, watching your staff prepare each batch recipe, and after they measure up an ingredient but before they dump it into the bowl, you need to say, "Stop! Weigh it." Then write it down.

When they go for the next ingredient, "Stop! Weigh it." Then write it down.

When they go for the next ingredient, "Stop! Weigh it." Then write it down.

When they go for the next ingredient, "Stop! Weigh it." Then write it down.

You get the picture.

You need to know with certainty. Not "generally" but without a shadow of a doubt.

You get your ingredients from Sysco, US Food, Ben E. Keith, Shamrock Foods, or whoever your broadline distributor may be. They give you the products, but you create something new with them. The only way you can control your costs is by keeping your numbers accurate.

When we talk about yield with batch recipes, it's how many usable ounces or portions you're getting from each batch recipe when you're finished preparing it.

For example, let's say you're making melted cheese dip. What's the recipe?

- 32 ounces of whole milk

- 160 ounces of casa white cheese

- 5 ounces of jalapeño vinegar

- 10 ounces of diced pickled jalapeños

- 0.3 ounces of salt

- 0.1 ounces of pepper

You take it all, dump it in a pot, melt it down, and let it cool—then put it into a Lexan for later. Before you put it away, you need to measure how many usable ounces you got from that recipe.

This way you can calculate the batch cost and use that to come up with the cost per ounce when you serve it. Let's say you take the $31.25 of product you started with and divided that by the 205 fluid ounces you have in finished product. This batch recipe breaks down to $0.15 per usable ounce.

Now, when you create a recipe costing card for pretzels, you know that when you add 2 ounces of cheese sauce, that will add $0.30 to your item cost.

Your nachos that use 4 ounces would add $0.60 from that item recipe.

When you look at things this way, it's clear that without batch recipe costing cards, you can't complete your item recipe cards. If you try to do it anyway, they'll either be incomplete or absolutely wrong.

Overall, the batch recipe process should only take about a week. Oh yeah, I forgot. You're too busy—so fine, I'll give you two weeks. Any more time than that is out of the question. Why? Because these are all dated products.

Your peppers and onions, soups and sauces, and the dressings you make need to be made and used every week. If not, they're going to spoil and turn into wasted money rotting away in the trash. Either that or you're selling crap to your guests, but I *know* you wouldn't do that!

So go ahead and let your chef know you'll be breathing over their shoulder for the next week or two. It's a pain in the ass for now, but you'll be a lot happier once you have your recipe costing cards on track.

Advanced Recipe Costing Strategies

Since I already told you that old-fashioned paper and pencil isn't good enough to get your recipe costing cards done correctly, there must be a better alternative, right?

What do you think I'm about to suggest? Spreadsheets?

Wrong.

While I teach most systems using spreadsheets, and I do this for recipe costing cards as well, the reality in today's day and age is spreadsheets barely get the job done. Things can change overnight. Prices fluctuate all the time. Today, you must have software helping you keep your menu on target. That's why, in the beginning, you can start by using spreadsheets to complete your recipe costing cards, but software to manage them will eventually be a must.

Putting Recipe Costing Cards to Work

With properly calculated recipe costing cards in hand, the real fun begins. That's when you can start positioning your restaurant to operate more efficiently. That's when you'll finally be in the right place to start making some real money.

Use your recipe costing cards to perform the menu engineering that'll increase your restaurant's profitability. They'll help you with things like

- identifying the best- and worst-selling items on your menu,

- recognizing the difference between COGS and your contribution margin,

- understanding the effects of menu mix, and

- creating menu scenarios to determine the menu changes that'll create the best results.

You'll have a better understanding of how your restaurant operates and, more importantly, where your money is going. Recipe costing cards are the golden tickets that help you stop using dumb-ass luck to make critical decisions.

> Recipe costing cards are the golden tickets that help you stop using dumb-ass luck to make critical decisions.

Maybe you need to do something as simple as change "mayo" to "chipotle mayo" on the item's description. Using my menu engineering process, one restaurant owner saw a six-point change on a $2.5 million restaurant. You can have that, too, but only if you get your recipe costing cards and menu mix in order first.

You've got to have recipe costing cards.

I speak at conferences and seminars all the time, and as soon as I get off the stage, there's always somebody waiting for me to say, "Hey, David, can you take a look at my menu for me really quick?"

The first thing I say back to them is "Do you have accurate, up-to-date recipe costing cards?"

If their answer is no, then my answer is no.

Recipe costing cards are part of the lifeblood of your business. Not only do they show you where you are and where your restaurant could be, they help you decide on the best way to reach your goals.

Are you going after lower food cost or higher cash contribution?

What's taking up space on your menu? If you're only selling one or two of an item each day, just get rid of it. Those customers who ordered it will probably be looking for that item you dropped off the menu, but they'll find something else.

If you got rid of the tuna salad, they will probably purchase the salmon salad, and it would be a better seller.

Maybe the change is as simple as switching from pine nuts to toasted sliced almonds instead. Do you need to rename the item or completely replace it? Don't guess. Tell me what your recipe costing cards say.

More than anything else, having recipe costing cards in hand will help you avoid another one of my industry pet peeves. I go freaking nuts whenever I hear that someone let a menu company do their menus for them just by asking what their top moneymakers are.

They never ask for your recipe costing cards. They just ask about your two top-selling items, and they merchandise the hell out of them. But what if one of those items had a 40 percent food cost because you weren't priced well enough because you *generally* knew what the protein costs were?

You could love the menu and be married to the design, but those blind menu companies could literally engineer your menu to put you out of business. If you don't devote the time to work through your recipe costing cards, you could lose money faster than ever before by having a third-party manufacture a menu that promotes the hell out of the wrong items.

Remember, without recipe costing cards, the analysis cannot be done. Don't wait! Get started on this forty-to-sixty-man-hour process so you can engineer a menu that makes you money every day!

If you want to make a change to your business—change that will ultimately make you more money, reduce your labor costs, and lower your food cost all at once—you need to get your recipe costing cards in order.

CHAPTER TAKEAWAYS

- You can't have accurate recipe costing cards without systems.

- Get in the kitchen and perform yield tests to know the actual cost of your inventory.

- Batch item recipes eliminate the guesswork in creating accurate recipe costing cards.

- Use the recipe costing cards to engineer your menu to arrange items that match your budget goals. Are you trying to lower your food cost or reach a higher cash contribution? Whatever your goals, you need recipe costing cards to achieve them.

CHAPTER 10

CALCULATING *YOUR* IDEAL FOOD COST

Your menu will determine the ideal food cost for *your* restaurant—forget you ever heard about an industry average. That has nothing to do with what goes on inside your four walls.

When you understand your own food costs, you can make the right decisions that affect the profitability of your business.

> Most restaurant owners run their businesses off average costs. The problem is your restaurant is not average.

Have you ever wondered about how small changes can impact your bottom line?

Your recipe costing cards hold all the answers.

Most restaurant owners run their businesses off average costs.

The problem is your restaurant is not average. You're not on the same street corner, serving the same item, using the same quality of products, or providing the same style of service. So if your restaurant is not average, then your food cost target should not be based on a national average.

Relying on a national average is the worst thing you could do.

You need to know where your food costs should be with no waste, theft, or spoilage—if you were operating like the perfect restaurant, which does not exist.

If you followed your recipe costing cards to the letter and your kitchen staff never let any usable ingredient find its way to the trash, where would you be?

Those industry averages don't account for restaurants serving high-end steaks versus the restaurants serving tacos. Therefore, you *must* calculate *your* ideal food cost. With that number in hand, you can make changes in your business that will make you a lot of money!

Calculating Target Ideal Food Costs

When it's time to break down your food costs, where should you start?

Let me share with you the way I was taught when I was a young manager. (Please note that it's 100 percent wrong!) I am sharing this with you now because I want to make sure you don't follow this path like many restaurants before you have.

So what you do is list out all the items on your menu in column A of a spreadsheet. Then in column B, the recipe cost; column C, the sales price on your menu; and column D, the food cost percentage, which is calculated as use divided by sales. Then total the cost column and the price column. Finally, calculate your ideal food cost of total use divided by total price.

Why is this wrong? Because it doesn't take into consideration what your customers purchased. Your ideal food cost is based on a nasty mathematical term called a weighted average. In the example above, it takes into consideration only one of each item sold. But the truth is you might have a frozen appetizer that goes directly from the box to the fryer and has a 38 percent food cost and you honestly don't sell many of them each day. But you also sell the heck out of your fresh, hand-cut french fries that have a 5 percent food cost. You will have items up and down your menu at different cost percentages, and your ideal food cost can only be figured out when you add how many of each item you sell.

Here's an oversimplified example.

Let's say you have a two-item menu—that's right, you only sell two items. Let's say one item has 1 percent food cost and the other has a 99 percent food cost; after selling one hundred items in a month, you realize ninety-nine sold at 1 percent and one at 99 percent. What's your food cost? One percent.

Next month, if you sold the same menu, this time with ninety-nine items at 99 percent and one item at 1 percent, where does that leave you? Ninety-nine percent.

See why the way I was taught (and many restaurant managers are still taught) is completely wrong?

The only way to evaluate how your menu is performing is to

1. have accurate and up-to-date recipe costing cards and

2. review your item-by-item sales mix report, also known as a velocity report, daily sales report, or product mix (PMIX) report, depending on your point-of-sales system.

Quick note: The PMIX report holds the key to your menu's

profitability, but I teach more about that in my course.

Once you have those first two steps down, you'll need to use a spreadsheet or a tool I created called the Restaurant Menu Profitability Monitor to learn what your ideal food cost is based on your recipe costing cards, sales prices, and what your customers actually ordered.

Once we have this information … powerful, profitable changes can be made in your kitchen and on your menu.

Measuring the Profitability of Your Menu

Why did I take you through that grueling breakdown on recipe costing cards in the last chapter? Because once you find the time to invest forty to sixty man hours into getting them done, you'll finally hold the key to real cost-savings power.

You need to know what *your* ideal food cost is for *your* menu— forget about industry averages.

Using the recipe costing cards, you can measure your chef or kitchen manager's performance and instantly drop your food cost five to seven points.

Cost. That's what this is all about.

You need to know what *your* ideal food cost is for *your* menu— forget about industry averages.

You need to know what changes you can make to your menu that will improve your costs and impact your bottom line.

Most restaurants run off an average food cost target they have learned from an industry publication or some praised keynote speaker. I can't wrap my head around the reason why, though. I just have to be honest. As I've explained, averages don't do anything for your restaurant because they're not taking a lot of costly variables into account.

You need to know where your specific restaurant's food cost should be so you can avoid industry hazards such as waste, theft, and spoilage.

Ideal food cost dictates what life would be like in the perfect restaurant. It's the cost outlined by following your (accurate) recipe costing cards.

Let your recipe costing cards help you understand your ideal cost (or theoretical food cost) so you know where you should be aiming.

Getting the Most Out of Your Food Cost Numbers

Ideal versus actual versus budgeted. That's the formula to remember.

Your recipe costing cards share the ideal cost of your menu when combined with the report that details what your customers actually ordered. Again, this represents what your food cost should be if you ran a perfect restaurant. (Again, we know that does not exist.) Based on your ideal cost, your kitchen would have done a great job running if your actual food cost was 1.5–2.0 percent higher than ideal because there is no such thing as a perfect restaurant.

Your budgeted food cost percentage comes from the budget targets you created for the next twelve months, which is based on your past and, ultimately, what systems you are going to put into place to achieve the percentage needed to make the money you deserve.

Your actual food cost is based on what left your shelves:

beginning inventory + purchase – ending inventory = use

Use divided by sales gives you your actual food cost percentage. This represents how much product you used, sold, or wasted or food that spoiled, was stolen, or was taken that wasn't rung up in the POS system against the food sales your brought in.

Why is it so important to measure your ideal versus actual costs? You need to know where your money is going. Comparing ideal and actual costs lets you know how efficient your kitchen is running. If the numbers are too far off, you'll know that you have a real problem executing in the kitchen and it's time to train your kitchen manager or chef on how to stay on target.

You're shooting for one and a half to two points over your ideal because there's no such thing as a perfect kitchen. Most restaurants operate four to ten points over ideal. There's always some level of theft, waste, or spoilage. If your actual ends up being under your ideal, your chef probably cheated on those recipe cards and padded them.

Why is it important to measure your ideal cost versus your budget? If your ideal cost isn't one and a half to two points below your budget, the only way you can make budget is to cheat your guests out of something by purchasing low-quality product or cutting back on portions. Comparing these two figures helps you decide where you need to reengineer your menu to lower ideal food cost, lower your labor cost targets, or change it to go after higher cash contribution.

Why is it important to measure actual cost versus budget? If your actual cost is higher than your budgeted targets, you will run a higher than budgeted prime cost and lose money. Looking at these numbers can help you reevaluate the systems you have in place, make sure they're actually being used, and retrain your people and hold management accountable to those systems.

If you check your systems and everyone's abiding by them to the letter, then disparities between actual cost and your budget probably means that you need new systems to help you achieve your numbers.

CHAPTER TAKEAWAYS

- Find *your* ideal food cost.

- Review your item sales mix report or the PMIX to measure your menu's profitability .

CHAPTER 11

DEVELOPING AN EFFECTIVE TRAINING PROGRAM

If you're in the hospitality industry and the goal is to create an unforgettable experience for every one of your guests, you need a team of people trained and prepared to fulfill that vision. What's the secret to finding these people and keeping them?

At the time of this writing, the country's unemployment rate has plummeted below 4 percent, and the reality is there aren't as many good people for you to recruit to your team. Once upon a time, there was a ton of talent just waiting to find a great restaurant home. Nowadays, you have to know how to create the people you want to keep around.

Great employees aren't hired; they're trained. In today's market, coming across a ready-made employee has become one of those tall tales we whisper over campfires while roasting marshmallows. I don't care what's on their résumé, where they used to work, or how great their knife skills are: every single person who comes to work in your restaurant needs to undergo intense training sessions.

You don't have room to leave anything to chance. Once you find an employee who may have what it takes, you have to take every precaution to make sure that person is properly introduced to the way you do things in *your* restaurant. And if you haven't guessed it yet, that starts with having the right systems.

That's right. Systems aren't reserved for day-to-day operations. You need a system to train people on the correct way to use your systems. Does that make sense? Just bear with me for a minute, and you'll see why this is so important.

First things first: with the right training system in place, you'll encourage those talented prospects to stick around. They're going to look at your restaurant and compare how organized and efficient you are to every crappy restaurant experience they had in the past. They're going to notice how much effort you put into building a team of competent, qualified people, and all inclinations toward pulling another round of NIGYYSOB will magically float away.

As soon as they step foot in the door, you have to set a standard for them. How well your employees are trained—from the back of the house to the front—will make or break your restaurant. Throw the systems at them right out of the gate. This will do one of two things: scare the bullshitters away so they can't cost you unnecessary time and money and inspire good workers to become great.

> During the hiring process, prospects stare you up and down and size you up in the same way you do to them.

During the hiring process, prospects

stare you up and down and size you up in the same way you do to them. You aren't the only one passing judgment at the interview table. Some people can spot a sucker from a mile away—systems take all emotion out of the hiring and training process. They place all your expectations in black and white and show how much you've invested into the success of your restaurant. I'm telling you now, if you put them into action, you're going to see a 180-degree shift in your restaurant's productivity and employee turnaround.

Years ago, I came across a study called "The Spirit of Service" done by the National Institute for the Foodservice Industry (NIFI). NIFI isn't around anymore, but the information they released in that study eventually became the platform for the way I explain the importance of training to other restaurateurs. I've met with my fair share of owners and managers who will try to reject the idea of implementing systems like the plague. Some think it's too much work. Some adopt that "if it ain't broke" mentality. Others just don't care. All objections aside, not one of them has ever argued against the numbers. "The Spirit of Service" detailed six main reasons why customers will walk out the door of your restaurant and never return. I don't care what happened to NIFI. This list is freaking timeless.

Every time a customer leaves your restaurant with no intention of returning, you sit and watch money walk right out the door. Without going into too much detail, let me share a quick CliffsNotes breakdown.

About 8 percent of the factors that take customers away from your restaurant are out of your control. But 82 percent of your customers cut ties because they came across an indifferent employee who left a sour taste in their mouth.

Here's how NIFI laid it out:

- 1 percent of your customers die,

- 3 percent move away,

- 5 percent find new interests and make new friends,

- 9 percent have a better experience with one of your competitors,

- 14 percent think your restaurant sucks, and

- 68 percent believe your employees don't give a damn about their jobs.

The first three things on the list are completely out of your control, but the last three are all about whether you can offer your guests an experience that makes them *want* to come back.

That's why proper training is so important.

I don't care if you're just training your staff to regain control of your restaurant or if you're trying to recoup a few percentage points. The journey is the same. It's no different than what I've been preaching to you all along. You need a system for every aspect of your restaurant.

It's easy to point fingers at your employees and throw your hands up in frustration, labeling everyone an idiot (or a millennial, as so many of the older restaurant owners I work with want to do). But are your people really idiots, or do they just not know what the hell they're supposed to be doing? Before you write them off as imbeciles, take a long, hard look in the mirror.

What example are you setting for your staff? Have you implemented processes and detailed systems that guarantee their success?

How many of your employees know what is expected of them during each shift, what they should be doing minute by minute, and what you would deem a successful shift? I'm willing to bet fewer than two.

To increase this number and your employees' success, you must have a painfully specific training program in place based on job descriptions. Doing so leaves no room for error.

Every employee deserves a job description. It provides clear expectations and gives them a guide on how to perform at the standard you've set. Remember, we're a long way away from suffering from common sense-itis. If you didn't give your employee a (detailed) job description before throwing them on the floor, how are they supposed to know what to do?

Because you told them? That never works.

Job descriptions give people a no-fail template and eliminate all excuses whenever it's time for a performance evaluation.

The job description erases "I didn't know" from your employees' vocabulary. They go a long way in demonstrating who's above the bar and who's struggling to keep up. And don't be mistaken: job descriptions help the owners and managers out too. At any given moment, there could be 101 things going on in your restaurant. Are you going to remember who you told to take out the trash when your kitchen's backed up with orders and customers are starting to get antsy? Probably not.

Do yourself a favor, and take one more thing off your to-do list.

Anybody representing your restaurant needs to know four major things:

1. what the job is,

2. how to do it,

3. how well it should be done, and

4. by when.

There are a lot of ways to look at the importance of training, but for the purposes of this discussion, let's take a bottom-line approach. If you aren't investing in a proper training program for your employees, it's costing you more than you think.

Your Employee Just Quit—How Much Did That Cost You?

Every time you lose an employee, you're losing money. Isn't that something?

I've already shown you how having crappy employees can scare your customers away and cost you lots of money in the grand scheme of things. Now I'm telling you that you're going to lose money if you get rid of those shitty people. I know you're thinking, "Well, David, what in the hell am I supposed to do?"

Start a better training program—one that relies heavily on systems. If those employees were properly screened and trained during the hiring process, they never would've had a chance to scare away your regulars with their nonchalant attitude, and they wouldn't be in your restaurant screwing up until they get fired or walk off the job.

Most people quit within the first ninety days. That's the typical probationary period and, in my opinion, more than enough time for someone to figure out they don't know what the hell they're doing. That was ninety days' worth of wages that came out of your pocket, ninety days of mistakes ... mistakes you'll be trying to fix for longer than ninety days after they leave.

I'm not a psychic, but I know what you're missing. Every day, somewhere in the world, another restaurant hires someone off the street, assuming they should know what they're supposed to do. A manager tosses an apron at their chest, then throws them to the wolves because common sense is something everyone has, right?

Absolutely not.

More often than not, that new employee will spend that first ninety days, give or take, on the job fumbling all over the place, trying to figure out what they're supposed to do while being managed by a bully (who is also not trained). Eventually, they hit a breaking point, and they walk off the job.

> Every day, somewhere in the world, another restaurant hires someone off the street, assuming they should know what they're supposed to do.

What's the first thing that comes to mind when someone quits your restaurant? You better be thinking, "I just lost $2,000." Heck, I've seen new studies that put this number up around $5,000 plus! Cornell University's School of Hotel Administration published a study called "The Cost of Employee Turnover: When the Devil Is in the Details" that breaks the expense down like this:

- -$176 on the predeparture,

- -$1,173 on recruiting,

- -$645 on selecting a new employee,

- -$821 on training, and

- -$3,049 lost in productivity.[4]

According to Cornell, the cost of *each* turnover is almost at $6,000! Other research is a little more modest, but generally speaking, every time you experience employee turnover, that's at least $2,000

---

4   J. B. Tracey and T. R. Hinkin, "The Costs of Employee Turnover: When the Devil Is in the Details," *Cornell Hospitality Report* 6, no. 15 (2006): 6–13.

taken out of your pocket. Lose five people in a month and your restaurant just flushed $10,000 down the toilet.

Add it all up:

- absenteeism,

- low productivity,

- workers' comp claims,

- uniforms,

- training wages (for them and the person who trained them),

- lost opportunity, and

- all the product they wasted because they didn't know what they were doing.

Having someone quit can easily become a hefty expense.

THE TRAINING PROCESS

I could write a second book just on restaurant training alone. You can't just drag a guy into a kitchen and point out the plates and the deep fryer. When creating a training program, you have to cover every base possible, including how to write job descriptions people can actually understand, how to make sure employees are ready for the floor or kitchen line, how to manage an employee who just doesn't seem to care, and how and *why* to promote from within. There just isn't enough room in this book to cover all of that. Don't worry, though. I won't leave you up the creek without a paddle. I am developing online courses to cover all these topics and more and will definitely include a series of online courses about restaurant employee training in the near future.

I know people need this information, and I want to make sure you get it in the right way. Until then, I really want to stress the importance of why you need to spend a good amount of time training everybody in your restaurant.

People need to be pushed to reach their full potential. They need to be inspired to be more than average, and that won't happen unless they're working in a restaurant with a success-driven culture.

Training isn't all about finding and hiring potential; it's also about the process of elimination. Some people just won't get it. Some people just won't fit in. Some people just don't need to be your employee.

CHAPTER TAKEAWAYS

- Eighty-two percent of your guests never come back because of a terrible experience with your employees.

- Every turnover costs you at least $2,000. It's much cheaper to train the right employees.

- You need a clear, complete job description and detailed training plan to help new hires be successful.

CHAPTER 12

WRONG LABOR TARGETS ARE COSTING YOU THOUSANDS

Now you have a better understanding of what poor hiring and training practices can cost you. You know how to pick the right people and promote those who prove they have the gusto to get shit done. But do you know how much your labor should cost you?

If you're operating with static labor targets (like most people), your numbers probably feel impossible to hit. After you've invested so much time into training your staff, the next thing you need to do is reconfigure your expenses.

In all my years, I've seen everyone take the same approach to labor control, and for the life of me, I can't figure out why the hell they throw money away like that. You know it well: the logic of "I'll bring everybody in just in case I need them, and if I don't, I'll just send them home."

Why? I mean, to be fair, I understand the intent behind it, but if you've been in business for even a few months, it isn't hard to see that this just doesn't work.

I get it. I know people do this because they want to make sure that they're prepared for the what-ifs. You want to be able to give your customers the best service and even better food. If things pick up, it's a lot harder to call people in to help out than it is to just pick somebody to clock out and go home when you don't need them. I get it, I really do.

However, there are two major flaws with this approach:

Flaw 1. When you overstaff your restaurant, you're actually providing *worse* service to your customers, not better. Think about it. When you have a bunch of people on the floor with nothing to do, what do they do? Servers start talking with each other and ignoring the guests. Now think about those times when your restaurant is busy. What are your employees doing?

Working. Like they should be.

Busy restaurants keep employees on their toes. They're paying attention to the guests. They're busy and don't have time to waste on catching up with their coworkers.

Busy restaurants keep people moving around, and in all honesty, people get a lot more done with that fire underneath their feet.

Flaw 2. The second flaw is if you decide to bring in seven servers at 4:00 p.m. on a Friday night and, three hours later, you realize that you're not going to be as busy as you thought so you start sending people home, it's *still too late.*

You've already lost money!

Every second those people stand in your restaurant with nothing to do sends money flying out of the window.

Changing the Way You See Your Labor Target

You have to start looking at labor differently. Yes, great customer service, appropriate ticket times, delicious food, and all that other Restaurant 101 stuff is important, but at the end of the day, you need to go to sleep with your hands folded behind your head and a smile plastered on your face because you know you made some good money.

How do you make sure you're making more money than you waste? You need a budget. (There's that dreaded word again.)

Budgets help you plan for success. They help you measure how successful your methods are and teach you how to be proactive when managing your business—rather than the reactive stance most owners take.

Why wait until you realize that you're going broke to decide to do something? Change the way you see your labor targets right now!

If your budget shows you that you need to be aiming for a 30 percent labor cost for the year, so that you can make some money, but maybe your in-season targets are 22 percent and a 35 percent labor cost in the off season, based on hitting your 55 percent prime cost for the year, you'll know

Without looking at your books, I can safely assume that anyone who doesn't have different target labor costs based on each month of sales is losing money.

that you're aiming for about 30 percent targets for the entire year.

But if you don't have a budget in place, you won't know any of that. You'll just keep wasting money like a dumb ass. Without looking at your books, I can safely assume that anyone who doesn't have different target labor costs based on each month of sales is losing money. Overstaffing will drain your profits little by little, and even after working through all the systems in the world—staying on top of your inventory, food costs, and all the other things we've discussed—without a budget, none of the rest of your targets will be as successful as they could've been.

Once you know where your targets are, budgeting for labor is so easy, and the success that comes after taking those few extra steps is really sweet!

So what does that mean for you? What do you need to do today to get your labor target budget down to a science?

1. You need an annual budget.

    This is a critical step. I mean, yes, you can budget labor without having an official budget laid out, but you'll leave a lot of money on the table if you skate past some of those crucial steps.

2. You must, I mean *must*, audit your timekeeping in whatever POS system you're using.

    Check and adjust your team's information in the POS, and make sure it matches what you have in your records. Pay attention to how much you're paying each employee. Make sure they're clocking in using the right job codes.

    For example, if you hired a cook at $10.00 an hour two years ago but they're currently making

$11.25, your payroll company will know about the switch, but is your POS system showing you the right hourly rate?

What about the employees who work in multiple positions? If they were hired to be a server making $5.00 an hour and got promoted to be a server trainer at $8.00 an hour, you need to make sure they're logging the right hours for the right position. The employee needs to be punching in and out using the right job codes for whatever role they're filling for any of what I am about to teach you to work.

Labor Budgeting for Success

With your budgets in place, it's time to start forecasting sales and keeping your timekeeping up to date. If you can handle that for one full work week (and I know you can), then you're ready to move on to the next step.

It's one thing to budget for labor; it's another to budget for success. I developed a labor budgeting system I refer to as the Restaurant Payroll Guardian that allows you to tell your management team how much money and how many hours they're allowed to schedule next week by position so that you can stay on budget. No more bring-them-in-and-send-them-home-if-you-are-slow business dealings. Now we're working on being proactive.

If you've forecasted your next week's sales at $50,000, you'll probably want to show maximum coverage for the week. Let's say your salaried managers, a fixed expense, get paid $3,000 a week and your total labor budget is 30 percent (not including taxes, benefits, and insurance, which would probably raise it to be a 35 percent labor target on your budget). With this information and an average hourly wage from last week, for *all* hourly employees combined, at $7.45 an hour, I'll show you how easy it is to go into next week on budget ...

Before I move forward, I want to answer one question that's probably floating around in your head right now.

"How can my average hourly wage of $7.45 work when I have servers who make $2.13 an hour in a tip credit state and cooks who get paid $15.00 an hour?"

It seems like it won't work, but it will because we tend to schedule the same people week after week on the same days, same shifts, including paying Jose overtime weekly so he doesn't get another job at another restaurant. We're creatures of habit. Your average hourly wage is actually a weighted average, which makes this process work. Watch me explain it now.

Step 1. Go to that expensive cash register called a POS system and run a labor summary report for last week. It is a report that summarizes your total regular hours and overtime hours worked and your total regular pay and overtime pay for last week by position. It should only take you a couple of minutes to find the report, run it, and print it.

Step 2. Grab your gross sales for that week.

Step 3. Calculate total hours worked, total pay, percentage of hours worked by position, average hourly wage by position, labor cost by position, overall hourly employee labor cost, and average hourly wages for the whole week. It should break down to something like the following chart.

LAST WEEK'S LABOR SUMMARY REPORT POS

Gross Sales: $40,000.00

POSITION	REG HRS	REG PAY	OT HRS	OT PAY	TOTAL HRS	TOTAL PAY	HR %	AVG WAGE	LABOR COST %
Server	632	$3,273.76	0	--	632	$3,273.76	45.6%	$5.18	8.18%
Bar	205	$1,697.40	0	--	205	$1,697.40	14.8%	$8.28	4.24%
Host	88	$528.00	0	--	88	$528.00	6.3%	$6.00	1.32%
Bus	52	$312.00	0	--	52	$312.00	3.7%	$6.00	0.78%
Cook	329	$3,699.54	20	$300.00	349	$3,999.54	25.2%	$11.46	10.00%
Dish	61	$518.00	0	--	61	$518.00	4.4%	$8.50	1.30%
Total					1387	$10,329.20	100.0%	$7.45	25.82%

Step 4. Calculate how many dollars and hours you have to schedule next week to be on budget.

How much money is budgeted for total labor?

Multiply your sales by the budgeted labor cost percentage.

> $50,000 forecasted sales
> × 30% budgeted labor cost (not including taxes, benefits, and insurance)
> = $15,000

How much money is budgeted for labor, less management?

> $15,000 total labor dollars
> – $3,000 manager salaries (fixed cost)
> = $12,000 labor dollars, less managers

How many hours can we schedule?

$12,000 labor dollars, less managers

÷ $7.45 average hourly wage from last week

= 1,610.7 total hours available for hourly employees

How many hours does each position get?

Multiply the total hours available by the hour percentage from last week.

Total hours: 1,610.7

Server	733.9	45.6%
Bar	238.1	14.8%
Host	102.2	6.3%
Bus	60.4	3.7%
Cook	405.3	25.2%
Dish	70.8	4.4%
		100%

Project the labor costs by position for next week by multiplying the allocated hours by last week's average hourly wage for each position from last week.

Step 5. Now that we know how many dollars and more importantly, how many hours we have to schedule, edit your schedule to meet the budget.

POSITION	WAGES	HOURS	AVG HRLY	LC %		
Server	$3,801.85	733.95	$5.18	7.60%		
Bar	$1,971.21	238.07	$8.28	3.94%		
Host	$613.17	102.20	$6.00	1.23%		
Bus	$362.33	60.39	$6.00	0.72%		
Cook	$4,644.71	405.30	$11.46	9.29%		
Dish	$602.14	70.84	$8.50	1.20%	Budgeted	Delta
Subtotal	$11,995.41	1,610.74	$7.45	23.99%	$12,000	$(4.59)

Simple, right?

Ah, don't be like that. All you need to do is write your schedule like you always do, making sure you take care of the needs of the business and the employees. Next, run your labor allotment to see where you need to be, to be on budget. Now compare the two!

Using the example above, you may find that you've scheduled 744 hours for servers and your labor allotment may say that you only get 734 hours. That means you would need to cut 10 hours from the server schedule, making sure you don't hurt service. How do you do that? Instead of bringing all your severs in at 4:00 p.m. on Friday to play grab ass at the POS terminal, only bring in two servers at 4:00 p.m. to set up the restaurant, one at 4:30 p.m., and the rest at 5:00 p.m.

This ensures you still have the seven servers needed to handle the business while reducing the amount of labor dollars being spent and maximizing your profits without hurting the guest experience. This system is simply magic!

I told you it works! (I bet you almost didn't believe me.)

While we're at it, let's talk about another benefit of looking at your labor targets this way: it gives you the power to start delegating the scheduling without giving up control of your checkbook. It's truly a win-win situation.

Your managers/supervisors write their schedules like they always do. You or your GM run the labor allotment on Monday afternoon. Your managers compare hours scheduled with hours budgeted and adjust their schedules, fifteen minutes here and fifteen minutes there even if it means adding more hours, until they match. Then they tell you to review the schedules. Now you don't have to micromanage the process and can ensure they are getting it done right and *on budget*. That's the most important part.

> You can't give a new manager a blank schedule and think they'll know what to do with it.

You can't give a new manager a blank schedule and think they'll know what to do with it. Staffing a restaurant and controlling labor cost requires explicit attention to detail. Every time somebody makes a mistake on your schedule, it costs you money.

Other tips of the trade I teach include

- scheduling two days off in a row,

- part-time employees and weak staff members lose their shifts first,

- keeping two more full-time employees than you need, and

- reminding your staff that scheduling requests are only requests, not a guarantee.

There's so much more for me to get into, but you'll find this information in my coaching program and video courses. For now, I want to leave you with the seven must dos to control your labor cost:

1. Make sure that your staff isn't clocking in too soon. With

proper planning and scheduling and periodic reviews of the POS system, you can stay on top of clock-ins before they get out of hand.

2. Make sure that staff isn't riding the clock. Pay attention to socializers and people milking the schedule.

3. Audit your timekeeping to verify that staff is punching in under the right job codes.

4. Audit your sales by the hour. Monitor the POS to track the beginning and end of your restaurant's rush. You need to know what's happening in your kitchen as much as what's happening out front.

5. Schedule staff according to the sales. Remember, your sales forecast needs to be arranged by the day of the week. Use it as a staffing guide, with at least three weeks of activity to identify a trend.

6. Avoid overtime at all cost. You're staffing for sales, not to bleed your budget. If anyone needs a schedule change, management must approve it ahead of time.

7. Make selection and training a priority. Poor selection is worse than being short staffed. Stop losing money on bad hires, and concentrate on developing a great training program.

CHAPTER TAKEAWAYS

- Labor cost is a crucial part of the prime cost equation.

- Use the POS system to help you schedule around demand.

- Monitor your schedule closely or else you'll keep losing money.

BUILDING A STRONG(ER) AND (MORE) EFFECTIVE MANAGEMENT TEAM

I asked a lot from you throughout this book. To be honest, there are umpteen volumes that I can add to this. Our industry is literally one of the toughest, most unforgiving, most cutthroat, and most *rewarding* you'll ever work in. I don't have to tell you that. I know that the growing pains of being an independent restaurateur can get a little overwhelming. But I also know stress doesn't have to suck all your love out of the business.

You just need the right systems, the right people, and the willingness to change. Before I let you go to start whipping your restaurant into shape, I want to bring your focus back to that second point for a minute.

What are you doing to make sure that you have the right people in your corner? How do you know who's worthy (and capable) of running your restaurant when you aren't around?

These aren't rhetorical questions. I really want you to think about them.

You need to know who you have in your company, who's representing your brand, and who's handling your customers. Why waste time waiting for blind perfection when you can literally breed rock star employees with the right systems supporting them?

> I need you working on your business, not holding hands with your employees while they set your bank account on fire.

Those are the kind of people you want to keep around. Those are your *implementors*.

I know I broke the word down, but now is when your management team really starts to matter. Now is when everything you decide to do, all the information you've gathered from this book, will either propel your business to profits you can only count in your dreams ... or drive you batshit crazy. But that'll only happen if you don't have the right people helping you facilitate this change.

I already told you what I want for you. I need you working on your business, not holding hands with your employees while they set your bank account on fire. Successful restaurants are managed and run by success-driven people. You need implementors handling the day to day while you're away doing your own thing. You need someone who'll walk in the door, know exactly what needs to be done, by when, and how to do it. You need a management team that's committed to getting shit done. It doesn't matter how big your restaurant is: the work doesn't change.

You need at least one key person to help you be successful. When I founded my restaurant coaching and training company in 2003, I spent way too much time trying to motivate the owners who came to *me* for help. All the cajoling, cheering, and scolding in the world couldn't get these owners to do the damn work. Then I realized a pattern. The entrepreneurial owners aren't interested in being consistent. They like adventure, challenges, and change. The clients who got the most done were the owners who had at least one implementor on their team.

Think about your staff. Who's the implementor on your team? I'm not asking about potential. I don't care what you think someone can do. I'm talking about a person who has the natural inclination to get shit done all day long. That's who you need to trust your business with.

They're the key person who

1. has already bought into your vision for success,

2. has been loyal to you and the business from day one,

3. has an amazing work ethic,

4. has no problem asking for help,

5. is engaged and asking good questions that help the restaurant grow,

6. sees the benefits of change without thinking of it as just extra work,

7. is *always* looking for ways to do things better than before, and

8. *takes action*!

This person isn't the company kiss ass. They aren't walking around the restaurant floor, strutting their feathers like a peacock. They don't care about titles; they care about results.

When you give the implementor a task, it gets done—every time.

By this point, that name you had in mind may have slowly started to fade away. Most people hear my breakdown on this crucial addition to your team and start scratching their heads in disbelief. They give me a puzzled look as if to say, "Do these kind of people really exist?"

They start thinking about the old managers and key employees they trusted in the past. The bittersweet taste of mixed success hits the tip of their tongue, and they start to shut down. "No, David— not again. I've tried that before. It never works."

That's because you didn't train them to reach their fullest potential. Let me share my number one tip for identifying the implementor in your restaurant and giving them what they need to be successful:

Let the candidates identify themselves.

I know you probably used to swear by it, but you cannot look at your people and eyeball who's got the best potential. I'll be fair and say a few managers could get lucky a time or two, but you already know how I feel about leaving your business to dumb-ass luck.

Don't.

Instead, let your implementors and managers in training show you who they are long before you ever start to interview them for the job. Here's a trick I like to use.

Post some stuff on your employee bulletin board, simple requests or special projects such as creating recipe costing cards, checklists, or setting up your inventory systems. Let them come to you. Pay attention to who raises their hand to do things outside of their job description. Look at who asks questions and starts to pick up tasks without being asked. You don't have to try to influence them. Don't suggest that your usual go-to employees head over to the board and check it out. Even better, don't count anyone out, even if you don't think they'll become the "chosen one." People can really surprise you when the opportunity presents itself.

It doesn't stop there. Raising their hand is a great start. Next, you need to see how well they perform the tasks. You have to see that this person has the skill sets and the work ethic to become the implementor or manager in training that you need.

Try it out and see what happens. You'd be surprised by who makes the cut. Sometimes, it'll be the person you least expect.

Worst case scenario, they step up and don't perform well. That's fine. They still get an A for effort ... and you know not to give that person any more special jobs. Not everyone is going to evolve into an implementor, and that's OK—as long as they know how to perform their job as trained and described.

Best case scenario, they knock it out of the park and you now know at least one person who has the gusto to become the implementor that'll help hold your restaurant together (with the help of the right systems, of course).

If you have a manager, you should be able to tell who the implementor on your team is after about two or three weeks of implementing your new systems. As soon as the systems go live, your managers are going to show you how well they adapt to change. They're going to prove whether they're capable of doing the work and helping other employees through the transition. We've all heard the phrase "actions speak louder than words." Either your managers are going to do the work or they aren't.

Regardless, you'll be able to sit back, observe, take notes, and adjust your roles and responsibilities accordingly. Tracking your progress won't be difficult at all, especially because you're going to have checklists and specific tasks that need to be accomplished before you can move on to the next objective. If they can't keep up, they can't continue to be a manager in your restaurant. Remember, this isn't a charity. You're in this business to make money. No matter how long you've had an employee on your team, if they can't keep up with your changes and adjustments, then that could be a sign that their time at your restaurant is probably coming to an abrupt end.

> If they can't keep up, they can't continue to be a manager in your restaurant. Remember, this isn't a charity. You're in this business to make money.

And I do mean abrupt. Remember how much money bad employees can cost you. Time is of the essence.

Swindled by a Saboteur

Before you burst through the doors of your restaurant and start promoting anyone who seems to be walking the walk, I want to point out an anomaly I've discovered after years of working with teams of people with different personalities. There have been times when I've come across people who could talk their way into the oval office. With that sly, yet convincing politician smile, they'll tell you everything you want to hear. Out of their mouths, they'll sound like an ideal implementor, but in reality, they are the total opposite. I call these people your saboteurs.

Have you ever been tripped up by a saboteur? I've seen so

many different people fill this role, but they all fall into one of four categories:

- **The excuse maker.** This manager tells you there's not enough time to do their job. The work is too hard. They "never did it like that before." They try to convince you that you're asking for too much and tell you about your own restaurant. Their main goal is to convince you that the process of implementation is unreasonably difficult and the juice isn't worth the squeeze. They need you to believe that the stuff we've been talking about isn't for your restaurant. You're different, and the old way was just fine.

- **The negative talker.** This manager isn't going to do the work at all. Their negative attitude kills the morale of the whole restaurant, and they're always questioning what's necessary. They think their way is best and are often too smart for their own good. This know-it-all approach helps fuel the saboteur's goal of shutting down the process of change as soon as possible. They'll make your transition into systems hard at every turn, making it impossible to get anything done. Then they'll get in the ears of everybody else on your team, and before you know it, everybody's coming to you to complain. I'll tell you one thing: negativity is definitely contagious.

- **The thief.** This manager steals time by dragging their feet. They delay every action they take, and at times, they may even be bold enough to physically steal money or inventory. To this manager, change *must* be stopped in its tracks. If not, they know they'll be caught. So the thief decides to scream the loudest and create a panic before any of your systems can go into effect.

- **Mr./Ms. Two Faced.** This manager is the greatest threat of them all. They'll smile to your face, say yes to your every request, and even appear to be excited about the changes you're about to make. But behind closed doors, they're dreading the thought of making the shift and then decide to do nothing at all. They only say yes to you because they think it'll keep you happy (and out of their hair). The two-faced manager ultimately understands that you probably won't hold them accountable to what you're asking them to do anyway, so they just sit back and ride the wave. They think they have you figured out already, so they'll already have their excuses handy whenever you go to question them. The only thing separating the two-faced manager from the excuse maker is the fact that they choose to stroke your ego and say all the right things.

I told you that you weren't the only one passing judgment in the interview, but those same silent employee evaluations will continue to take place long after you hire them. That's why it's so important for owners to identify their leadership style so they can predict the types of hustles their employees may try.

Don't let people pull the wool over your eyes in your own restaurant. It's time to start viewing your employees differently.

Are they helping you grow or costing you money?

Are they backing up their words with actions or just blowing hot gas?

Are they showing you their potential without you even having to ask?

Are you ready to start making the money you deserve, or are you OK with seeing your profits bleeding red?

I know you're ready. I know you're going to take everything I just shared in the last twelve chapters and use it to turn your independent restaurant into a well-oiled machine. Even better, I'm willing to continue my commitment. Come to me with your questions. Let me help you succeed. With every new restaurant operator I encounter, I'm reminded of myself and my own journey. I think about my family and the little empire we've built together. I think about all the mistakes I've made and where I am now.

That's why I do what I do. And that's why I've shared the Restaurant Prosperity Formula with you.

ABOUT THE AUTHOR

David Scott Peters is a restaurant expert who teaches restaurant operators how to cut costs and increase profits with his trademark Restaurant Prosperity Formula. He's taught thousands of restaurants how to use operational systems and create a hospitality-based company culture to skyrocket their profits. He travels the world teaching his formula to restaurant owners, food distributors, and a variety of hospitality groups. In his past businesses, he has used his formula to rescue a multiunit restaurant/sports bar chain from bankruptcy and helped the owners sell it for a profit. He built a restaurant management software from the ground up based on his formula and sold it to a group of investors who included satisfied software users. To learn more about David's formula and sign up for tips, visit davidscottpeters.com.

A SPECIAL THANK YOU...

To my wife, Susan: Thank you for your support over the last twenty-two years (and counting). I know that being married to an entrepreneur can be much like riding a roller coaster. There are a lot of ups and downs and blind, scary corners; things can move way too fast; and there is an inherent risk taken just getting on the ride. I am most thankful to have you by my side, holding my hand through every scary moment and sharing in the thrills of success. Thank you for always encouraging me to follow my heart and make my dreams a reality. I love you, always and forever.

To my children, Tyler and Brooke: Thank you for teaching me that there is more to life than work and for never letting me take myself too seriously. My greatest joy in life is being your dad.

To my mom, Linda: Thank you for being my role model and teaching me that anything is possible. You have always been my biggest cheerleader. I wouldn't be where I am today without you.

To my dad, Howard: Thank you for inspiring me to follow in your footsteps as an energetic and passionate speaker from the stage.

I miss you every day and hope you're looking down from heaven proud of everything I've accomplished.

To my stepfather, Willis: Thank you for always being there for me and suggesting I apply to teach at the Scottsdale Culinary Institute with you. That one decision allowed me to find my real passion for teaching others how to run a profitable restaurant.

To my sister, Ami: Thank you for teaching me that everything starts with a dream, that your path is never a straight line, and that you should never make decisions based on what you think others will think about you.

To Jenny Brooks, who for the past fifteen years has been my copy editor, booking agent, and marketing partner, as well as the greatest evangelist I could ever ask for: Thank you for everything you do to support me. You have made it possible for me to share my knowledge with literally thousands upon thousands of restaurant professionals all over the globe, to change people's lives, and to put them on the path of having a life and making the money they deserve. I couldn't do it without you.

To the restaurant owners and managers who have been a part of my Elite Coaching Group over the last fifteen years: Thank you from the bottom of my heart. It was an honor that you trusted me to teach, help, coach, and consult you and your teams. What I cherish the most is the close bonds and friendships we have forged. I want you to know that I will always be in your corner. While I started out on this journey way back in 2003, calling myself an expert, I never realized how much I still had to learn. You all have taught me more than you can imagine and inspire me every day to share my knowledge with others so that they can have the same success as you.